HOW TO RECREATE YOUR OWN ANTIQUE
BEARS AND DOLLS

HOW TO RECREATE YOUR OWN ANTIQUE
BEARS AND DOLLS

Georgina Ledlie

ROBERT HALE • LONDON

All dolls and bears featured in this publication have been
individually handcrafted by the author

Note: *All patterns in this book are reproduced half size.*
They must be enlarged before use.
1 cm (⅜'') seam allowances included
on all patterns.

Robert Hale Limited
Clerkenwell House
Clerkenwell Green
London EC1R 0HT

Printed and bound in Hong Kong

Contents

Introduction

If you have a hankering to fashion your own doll or bear, help is at hand! There are other books, scores of them, some attractively illustrated in brilliant colour, some presenting the history of doll and bear making, several offering instructions using the conventional 'how to' approach. Each book in its own way is a competent teacher but, regrettably, many of them lack one fundamental ingredient. They lack excitement.

There is a fine but distinct line dividing the artisan and the artist. The former is one skilled in a trade, the latter practises an art form. There is a subtle difference. Putting a doll together, or a bear for that matter, must not be just a simple work project. It must be one that is to be enjoyed, savoured, petted and caressed, taking a collection of dull, inanimate materials and moulding them into something pulsating with life and character. This craft is for the artist, not the artisan.

My book, which is based on this concept, is a radical departure from the ordinary. The underlying intent is to recreate and recapture the magic and artistry of the old doll and bear makers using, as far as possible, the same old materials and techniques they used.

I have individually handcrafted each doll and bear in this book; the directions I have given are based on the special techniques relevant in each case. They should be followed closely and every attempt should be made to obtain the suggested old materials and other bits and pieces, even though there may be, at times, a delay in getting the project started. It is well worth the wait!

Remember, originals are rare and hard to come by; those that happen to be available are extremely expensive and generally beyond the means of the ordinary doll or bear collector. Here now is the opportunity to experience the pleasure and excitement of recreating some of the works of the old masters.

Georgina Ledlie

DOLLS

1 Izannah Walker Doll

Illustrated on page 33

IZANNAH WALKER

A well known early American dollmaker, Izannah Walker began her dollmaking career in 1855. Since then she has been regarded as the pioneer of the American cloth doll.

Walker used oil paints to finish the head, a special feature of her work being two sausage-type curls in front of each ear, with curls at the back. A centre part was used in most of her creations, reflecting the type of hairstyle common to women brought up in the rural areas of the United States. Her clothes for both boy and girl dolls were, in the same way, designed to conform to the children's fashions common to that period. For fabrics, she used soft cottons and homespun wool.

Hand-stitched fingers and toes, the feet occasionally covered by shoes and socks, were another interesting feature of her individual technique.

Izannah Walker originals are rare. Some do surface from time to time and should an opportunity to buy one arise, be prepared to pay US$25 000 or thereabouts.

An Izannah Walker doll head is made of moulded papier-mâché with a fine T-shirt fabric stretched and glued over the surface. Ready made commercial head moulds are available from craft stores (just separate the two halves) but you may prefer to make your own mould from the instructions below. Either way, the resulting head should measure approximately 33 cm (13'') in circumference.

Homemade head mould

Materials required
doll's head
polystyrene foam ball
strong cardboard box
potter's clay
Mould Release
potter's plaster
large artist's brush
large mixing bowl
water
wooden spoon or spatula

An old discarded doll's head will do the job. If you are using a modern plastic head, any rooted hair must be shaved off completely and any openings (bottom of neck, eyes) must be blocked off. If you are using a porcelain head, you will find that the top of the head is usually hollow. Eye and neck openings must be blocked off using potter's clay.

Plug the eye openings from the inside, most easily done with your fingers through the head opening, although it can be done through the neck. See Fig. 1.

To fill the head opening, use half a polystyrene ball of an appropriate size (from any craft store) and glue it on securely. See Fig. 2.

The cardboard box should be approximately 30 cm long, 25 cm wide and 23 cm deep (12'' × 10'' × 9''), which will allow for about 7.5 cm (3'') of clay/plaster surrounding the doll's head. See Fig. 3. Have a spare box the same size available in case the first one is destroyed during the moulding process.

Clear a work space and ensure that everything needed is at hand. Plaster hardens very quickly so one must work fast.

Directions

1. Using a felt-tipped pen, mark a line around the doll's head from the bottom of the neck, behind the ears, around the top of the forehead and down the other side. This is referred to as the 'parting line'. See Fig. 4.

2. Put a layer of clay about 7.5 cm (3'') thick into the bottom of the cardboard box. Lay the doll's head in the centre of the box, facing upwards. See Fig. 5.

3. Continue filling the box with clay up to the parting line. The clay fill *must not* go beyond the line. Level and smooth the clay around the head, ensuring that there are no gaps where liquid plaster could seep through and mix with the clay.

4. Using a large brush, paint the entire head, the clay surface and the inside walls of the box with Mould Release. Use this material generously.

5. Working quickly, mix a large quantity of plaster, following the directions on the packet. The trick is to add plaster to water (not the other way around), adding small quantities at a time and mixing continuously until all lumps have disappeared. The consistency should be similar to pouring cream or custard.

The mixing process should be completed with all possible speed as the plaster tends to set rather rapidly.

Pour the plaster into the box, starting at one corner and adding plaster until the entire head is covered to a depth of at least 7.5 cm (3''). Tap the box gently at the sides until all air bubbles have been eliminated. Allow to set. It takes approximately 24 hours for this much plaster to dry, depending on weather conditions. As the plaster begins to dry, it is quite warm to the touch, but it cools off as it hardens and dries.

6. When the plaster is completely dry and set, turn the box upside down and remove both the box and the clay, which should come away quite easily if sufficient Mould Release was used. Place the plaster back in the box. Occasionally a cardboard box will disintegrate. Should this happen, remove the plaster mould carefully and place it in another box of a similar size. The clay can be re-used if placed in an airtight bag.

7. The back of the head will be visible with the face embedded in plaster. Brush the back of the head, the plaster surface and the inner sides of the box generously with Mould Release. Prepare a further quantity of plaster mix and pour it into the box as before, tapping the sides of the box to remove all air bubbles. Allow to set.

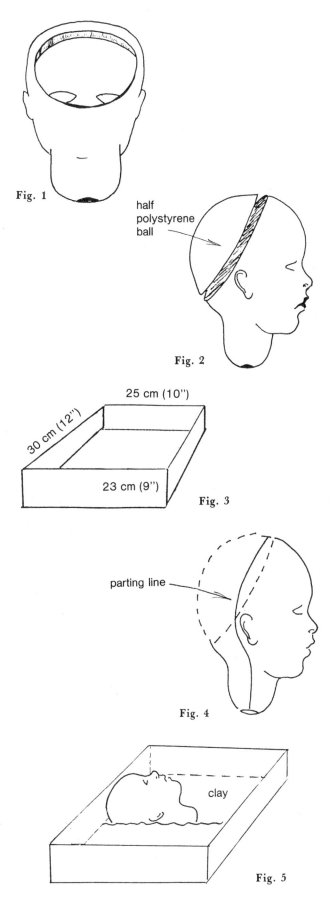

Fig. 1

half polystyrene ball

Fig. 2

25 cm (10")

30 cm (12")

23 cm (9")

Fig. 3

parting line

Fig. 4

clay

Fig. 5

8. The *entire* plaster cast must be *absolutely dry* before any attempt is made to separate the mould into its two segments and remove the doll's head. Sometimes it may be difficult to prise the two segments of the mould apart even though the join around the mould is clearly visible. Insert a sharp knife into the join, tapping gently with your hand, and work around the mould. The two segments should come apart. If they don't, transfer the whole sorry mess to the local council dump and buy a ready made mould from a craft store—unless you have the patience to have another go!

Caution   Do not pour any unused plaster down the kitchen sink. Your plumber's bill to sort out the resulting problem could be a headache!

Making the head

Materials required
Vaseline
instant papier-mâché (available at any craft store)
craft glue
mixing bowl
fine sandpaper
sharp craft knife

1. Mix papier-mâché as directed on the packet and put aside.

Cover the two separate moulds for the back of the head and the face with a layer of Vaseline. Use your fingers and cover all areas carefully, especially the nose, mouth and ears. Using small quantities, press the papier-mâché into the mould to an overall thickness of approximately 6 mm (¼″). Allow to dry.

Papier-mâché takes longer to dry than some other substances. If a measure of impatience creeps in after two or three days, pop the moulds into a very slow oven for a while—but keep an eye on what's going on so that the papier-mâché doesn't burn to a crisp!

When both sections of the head are dry remove them carefully from the moulds and wipe off any excess Vaseline. Trim the edges so that they fit together exactly, with no gaps, and bond the two sections together securely with craft glue. See Fig. 6.

Should gaps appear, mix a further small quantity of papier-mâché and plug them.

When completely dry, sandpaper the entire head until the surface is smooth to the touch.

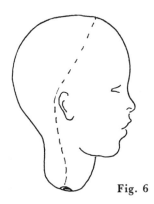

Fig. 6

The basic foundation for the doll's head is now complete.

2. Trace enlarged pattern piece for head (page 12) and cut out shape from a piece of T-shirt fabric. Brush craft glue over the entire head and face, ensuring that the material is pressed firmly into all crevices such as sides of the nose, mouth, inside and behind the eyes and under the chin. The fabric must follow all the contours of the face both accurately and completely.

Bring the fabric round to the back of the head and fold the edges in to fit. Some fabric may need to be trimmed off. Make a seam from the bottom of the back of the neck straight up to near the top of the head. Two or more additional seams may be needed from the forehead to the middle seam to fit the fabric neatly and securely to the head. Sew by hand with small neat stitches. See Figs. 7 and 8.

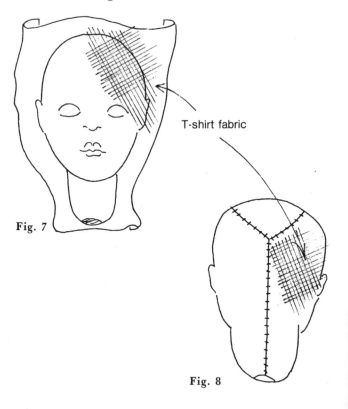

T-shirt fabric

Fig. 7

Fig. 8

Putting the body together

Materials required
0.75 m (30'') calico
stuffing (soft toy stuffing, straw, cotton wool, etc., available from any craft store)

1. Trace the enlarged pattern pieces from page 13 and cut out in calico. Make up and stuff all sections firmly. Fit the neck into the body section and sew firmly into place. See Fig. 9.
2. Stuff arms and legs up to the stuffing line and sew across the stuffing line. Sew lines of stitching on hands to denote fingers, stitching right through from front to back. See Fig. 10.
3. Make a small hem at the open end of each arm and leg. Sew by hand to the body. Ensure the thumbs point towards the body. See Fig. 11.

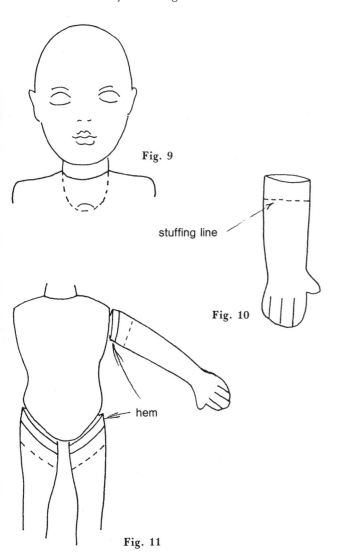

Fig. 9

stuffing line

Fig. 10

hem

Fig. 11

Painting the doll

Though the original Izannah Walker dolls were painted with oil paints, I find it preferable to use acrylic paints, if for no other reason than the question of time. Oils tend to take 5–6 weeks to dry out completely. Use the photograph on page 33 as a guide to painting the doll's face and hair.

1. Paint the entire face, ears and shoulders with a flesh coloured paint. Paint the arms up to the elbows with the same colour.
2. While the painted face is still wet, apply blush (cheek colour), preferably an orange-coloured tint. Apply the blush to the upper part of the cheek, below the eyes. Brush across towards the ears, the procedure being somewhat similar to making up one's own face.
3. Using white, paint in the eyes following the contours of the face. Unless you are an accomplished artist, it is helpful to lightly pencil in the outline before attempting to paint. Outline the eyes with a thin dark brown line and add another dark brown line above the upper line to form an eyelid. See Fig. 12.

Fig. 12

4. Paint a black circle inside the white area. Allow to dry. Using the iris colour of your choice, paint over the black, leaving just a very fine black line around the outside. See Fig. 13.

Fig. 13

5. When thoroughly dry, paint a small black circle inside the coloured area for the pupil. See Fig. 14.
6. Using a lighter shade of the iris colour, paint a crescent shape just below the black circle. See Fig. 15.

Fig. 14

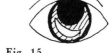

Fig. 15

7. Paint a tiny white dot at the upper left hand corner of the black circle. See Fig. 16. Pupil, crescent and spot must match in both eyes.

8. Shade in the corners of the eyelids with dark brown paint, using the same colour to form the eyebrows. See Fig. 17.

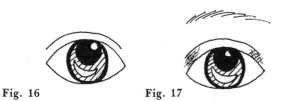

Fig. 16   **Fig. 17**

9. Place an orange dot in each nostril. Using an orange-red colour, paint the contours of the mouth, finishing the outline with a darker colour.

10. Hands and arms may be contoured in a similar manner if you wish.

11. The hair on an Izannah Walker doll is always centre parted, with two or three sausage-like curls in front of each ear. Use black paint. See Fig. 18.

12. Finally, apply two or three coats of quick-drying craft varnish over the entire head.

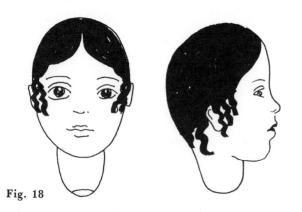

Fig. 18

13. Since an antique look is desirable I suggest an additional treatment to the face and hands. Brush them liberally with an ordinary dark brown timber varnish, diluted by mixing with a varnish thinner for a lighter shade and consistency. Experiment with the proportions before you paint the doll and try out the 'antiquing' on a spare piece of painted T-shirt fabric. While the varnish is still damp, buff gently with a soft cloth and allow to dry.

14. Use enlarged patterns from pages 14–15 to dress the doll.

PATTERNS FOR IZANNAH WALKER DOLL

Note: Enlarge all patterns to correct size by photocopying at 200%, *OR* enlarge by the grid method at 1 cm = 2 cm (½″ = 1″).

Seam allowance of 1 cm (⅜″) is included on all pattern pieces.

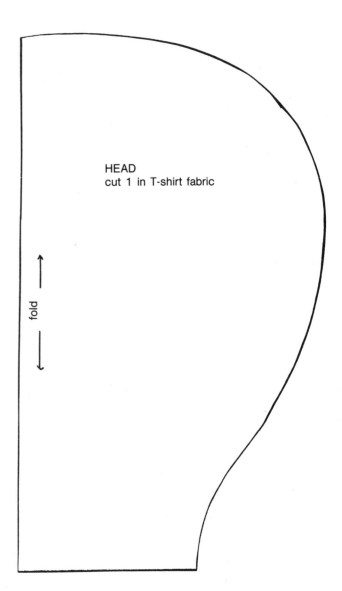

HEAD
cut 1 in T-shirt fabric

fold

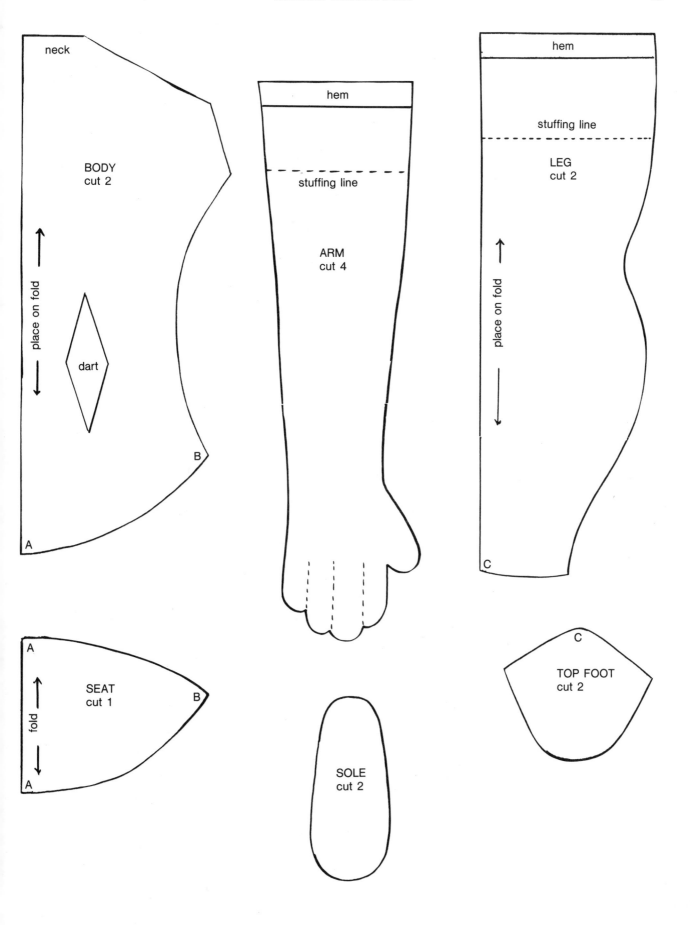

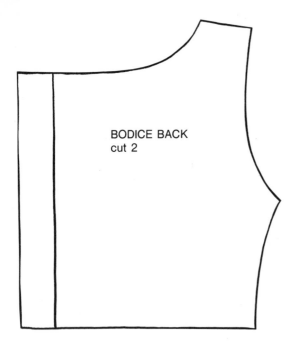

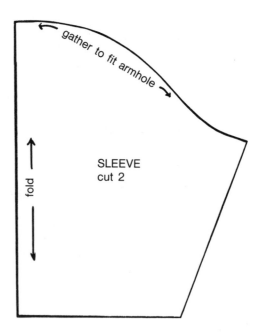

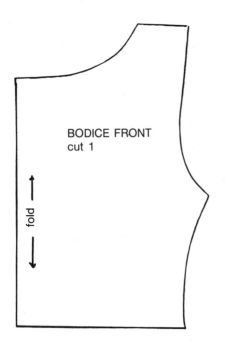

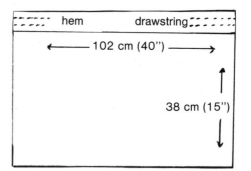

PETTICOAT GUIDE
cut 1, **following measurements** for size, not the diagram

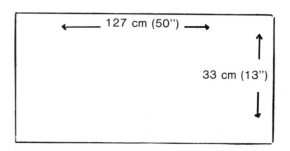

SKIRT GUIDE
cut 1, **following measurements** for size, not the diagram

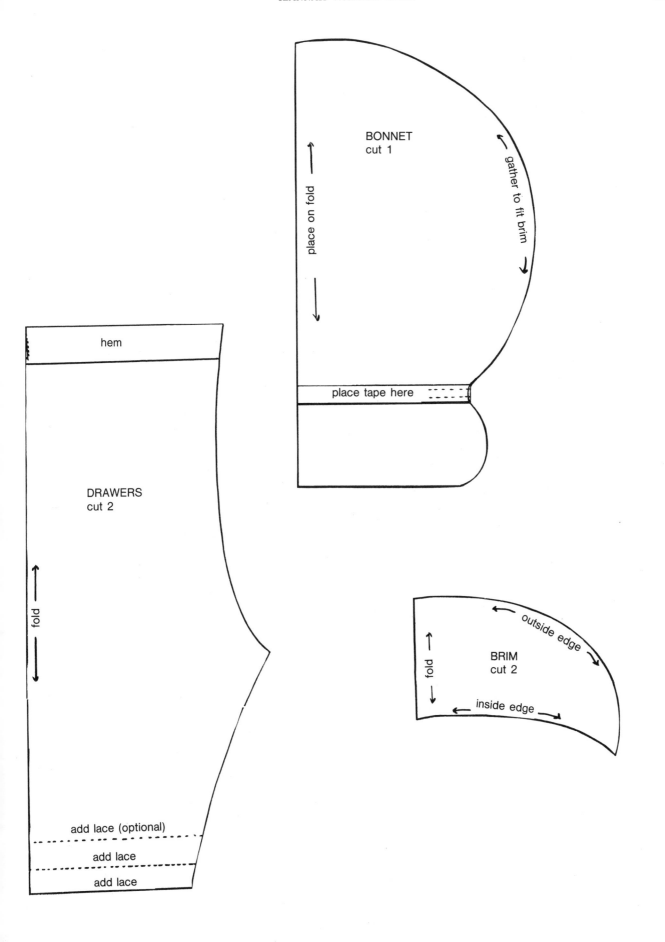

BONNET
cut 1

place on fold

gather to fit brim

place tape here

hem

DRAWERS
cut 2

fold

add lace (optional)

add lace

add lace

BRIM
cut 2

fold

outside edge

inside edge

2 Käthe Kruse Doll XII

Illustrated on page 34

Illustrated on page 34

KATHARINA KRUSE

Katharina Kruse was born Katharina Simon in Breslau in 1883. Acting lessons at 16 led to a successful career on the stage and at the age of 19 she met and married Max Kruse, a well known Berlin sculptor and author. In the course of this marriage she had seven children (the eighth died at birth) which naturally enough forced her to give up acting and assume a new role as a mother. It was her husband who suggested she make dolls for the children, pointing out that those that were available at the time, which were made from porcelain, were breakable and therefore quite unsuitable for children.

Her first doll was made in 1906. The head was a potato, the body was a knotted handkerchief filled with sand and the eyes and mouth were outlined with a burned match. This she continued to do until 1910, at which time, while in Munich, she acquired a bust of a child's head fashioned by a Flemish sculptor. Using this head and assisted by her husband, who was himself a sculptor, she succeeded in making her own mould and abandoned the use of a potato.

The base materials used by Kathe Kruse for the head, though they remain a trade secret, would have been either magnesite, hard rubber, cardboard or, perhaps, papier-mâché with a final fabric covering.

In 1911 she was invited to participate in a Berlin department store toy exhibition. This venture, her first foray into the public arena, proved very successful and not long afterwards she received her first order from the United States. Further orders followed regularly, in addition to several from Europe. To take care of this increasing demand she established a workshop in 1912 which was extended progressively in the years ahead as business continued to grow.

The demand for Käthe Kruse dolls and the quantities that had to be produced led inevitably to the loss of much of their originality, although it must be pointed out that they remained altogether distinctive and recognisable, primarily because the methods used in painting the eyes and mouth did not change over the years.

It is on record that Kruse designed dolls for children using the 'child for a child' philosophy. Soft and durable dolls became a feature of her work.

Käthe Kruse died at the age of 85.

Käthe Kruse dolls were numbered in order as new models were produced. Doll XII is perhaps one of the easiest dolls to reproduce as work on the body is relatively simple. The arms are attached loosely to the body and the legs are chubby with stiff soles and stitched toes.

Faces were entirely hand-painted using oils. The mouth was painted in an unusual style, the upper lip being a single line bow without the customary centre depression. Most of the early dolls were made from the same mould and the visual difference between one doll and another lay in the colours used in painting the face. The type of clothing showed whether the doll was a girl or a boy. Most dolls were dressed in cotton or knitted woollens with a bonnet or a hat made from raffia.

Head mould

To make a head mould follow the procedure described on pages 8–10 for the Izannah Walker doll. In this case, however, the doll's head used to fashion the mould must be that of a child doll. The same size, 33 cm (13''), is recommended.

Putting the body together

Materials required
1 m (1 yd) calico or any other flesh coloured fabric
stiff cardboard 15.25 cm (6'') square
stuffing—straw or cotton wool

1. Using the enlarged pattern from page 19 cut out body pieces from calico or other fabric.
2. Place the body pieces right sides together and sew up, leaving the neck open for stuffing. Stuff firmly but smoothly, ensuring that there are no lumps. Fig. 1.

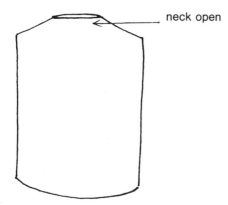

neck open

Fig. 1

3. The legs on the Käthe Kruse Doll XII are quite chubby with hard soles and stitched toes. Cut out all leg pieces from calico.
4. With right sides together sew up the centre front seam only.
5. Take the two side sections of the back pieces and sew them to the sides of the front of leg. Fig. 2. The result should resemble Fig. 3.

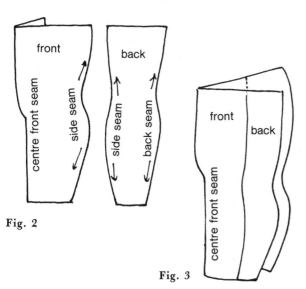

Fig. 2

front

centre front seam

side seam

back

side seam

back seam

front

back

centre front seam

Fig. 3

6. Flatten out the leg piece and place the centre of the upper foot (marked C) to centre (marked C) of leg front at ankle and sew together. Fig. 4.
7. Sew up centre back seam. Fig. 5.
8. Cut out two inner soles from thick cardboard. Glue one to each calico sole. Fig. 6. Allow to dry. Make a neat hem on to the foot. Do this by hand. It will be a lot easier if you begin to stuff the foot at the same time. Stuff to the top, fold over and close. Fig. 7.

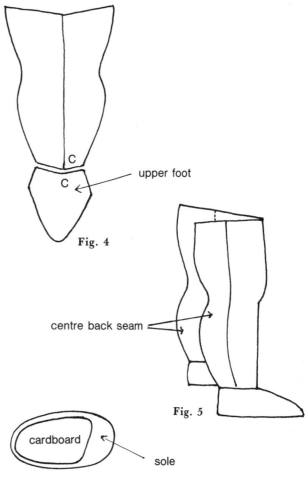

C

C

upper foot

Fig. 4

centre back seam

Fig. 5

cardboard

sole

Fig. 6

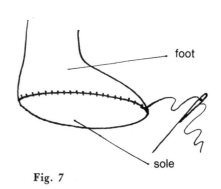

foot

sole

Fig. 7

9. Following the enlarged pattern from page 20, cut out two pieces of fabric for the upper leg. Sew into tubes and attach to legs. Hand stitching is recommended. Make a narrow hem and sew to body. See Figs. 8 and 9.

10. At the front of the foot there is an area with no cardboard underneath which becomes the toes. Using strong thread, hand stitch the outline of the toes. Fig. 10.

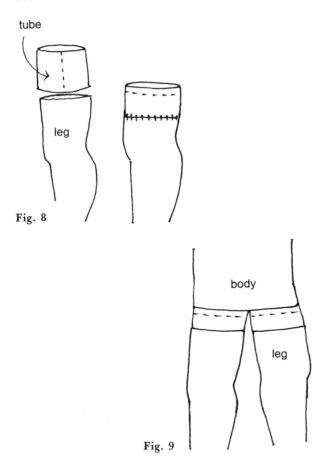

Fig. 8

Fig. 9

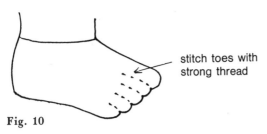

stitch toes with strong thread

Fig. 10

11. Cut arms from pattern, place right sides together, sew and stuff to stuffing line. Stitch across stuffing line and neatly attach arms to body. Sew lines of running stitch between the fingers, starting at the base of the fingers and stitching right through the fabric and stuffing. Figs. 11 and 12.

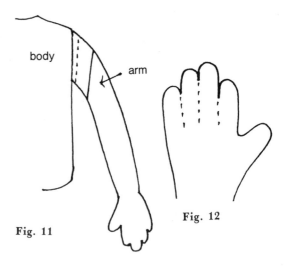

Fig. 11

Fig. 12

Painting the head

Materials required
paints (oils or acrylics) in Indian red, brown, black, white, coral and flesh
colourless varnish
brushes

1. Paint the entire head a flesh colour.
2. Blush the cheeks with a coral colour while the flesh paint is still wet. This helps the colours to blend.
3. The eyes on most Käthe Kruse dolls had radiating irises, which can be painted in quite easily following Fig. 13. The fine white lines are painted in last. Study the photograph on page 34 too.

Fig. 13

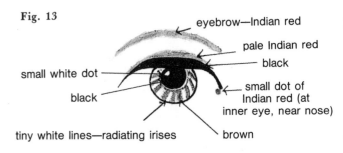

eyebrow—Indian red

pale Indian red

black

small white dot

black

small dot of Indian red (at inner eye, near nose)

tiny white lines—radiating irises

brown

4. Käthe Kruse dolls have no depression in the curve of the upper lip. Use a coral shade. Fig. 14.

Fig. 14

Fig. 15

5. For the hair, follow the style of the earlier dolls, which had painted hair. Using a brown shade, paint with light strokes across the forehead and above the ears. Allow to dry completely. Fig. 15. Varnish the entire head with two coats of quick-drying varnish.
6. Finally, attach head to body by hand.

PATTERNS FOR KÄTHE KRUSE DOLL XII

Note: Enlarge all patterns to correct size by photocopying at 200%, *OR* enlarge by the grid method at 1 cm = 2 cm (½'' = 1'').

Seam allowance of 1 cm (⅜'') is included on all pattern pieces.

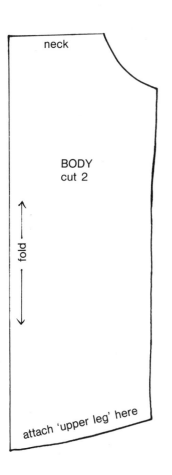

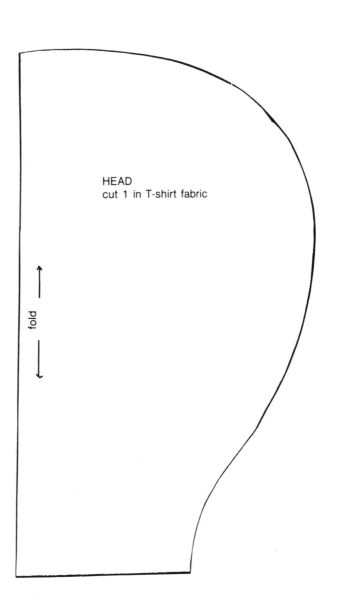

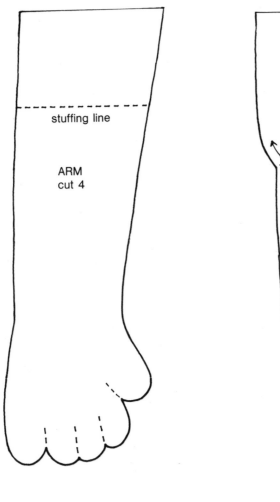

stuffing line

ARM
cut 4

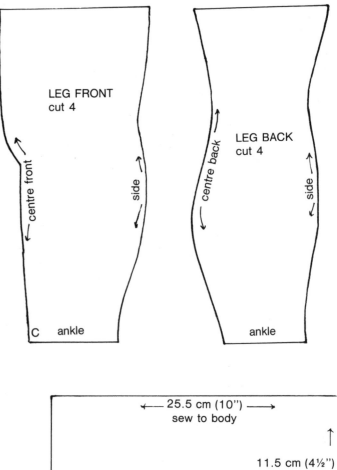

LEG FRONT
cut 4

centre front

side

LEG BACK
cut 4

centre back

side

C   ankle

ankle

←— 25.5 cm (10") —→
sew to body

↑

11.5 cm (4½")

↓

←— sew to leg —→

UPPER LEG GUIDE
cut 2, **following measurements**, not this diagram

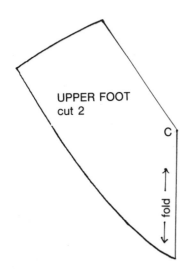

UPPER FOOT
cut 2

C

fold

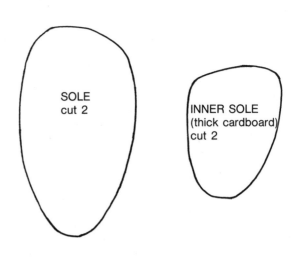

SOLE
cut 2

INNER SOLE
(thick cardboard)
cut 2

3 Käthe Kruse Träumerchen

Illustrated on page 35

Träumerchen (Sleeping Baby)

The first baby doll appeared in 1925, essentially intended to teach baby care. It had closed eyes, as the idea was to produce a doll which would resemble a newborn baby as closely as possible. (A similar doll was produced shortly afterwards—it had open eyes and was called the Du Mein.) In later years, both were produced as play dolls.

The doll was 50 cm (20'') tall and weighed 2.5 kg (5½ lbs). It had a cloth head and featured bags of sand distributed within the body to simulate the approximate weight of a newborn child. Because of this it was nicknamed the Sandbaby. Later on the sand bags were discarded and replaced with lead weights.

The head was left heavy and loose and had to be supported, not unlike a real baby, so that it lay comfortably in the holder's arms. For added effect a navel was sewn to the body.

Early Träumerchen models, those with cloth heads, are of continued interest to collectors, who must be prepared to meet a price in excess of US$2000. Subsequent models, those from 1935 on, have magnesite heads and are valued in the region of US$1000.

Making the head

Once again a head mould is needed. Follow the procedure outlined on pages 8–10, using a slightly larger head with a circumference of 34–35.5 cm (13½''–14'').

Put finished head aside.

Putting the body together

The Träumerchen is constructed of an inner body of calico covered by an outer skin of T-shirt fabric.

Materials required
0.5 m (½ yd) calico
0.5 m (½ yd) flesh coloured T-shirt fabric
stuffing
brushes—one wide, one fine
paints—flesh, brown, coral (oil or acrylics)
fine sandpaper
craft glue (optional)
quick-drying varnish

Inner calico body
1. Cut out pattern pieces for the inner calico body. Place the right sides of the body pieces together and sew. Leave neck open. Fig. 1.

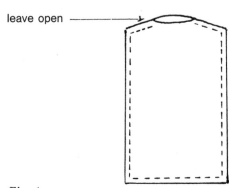

leave open

Fig. 1

2. Sew the two centre fronts of legs together. Sew the side fronts to the side backs. Leave the back seam open. Figs. 2 and 3.

3. Sew upper foot section to leg, matching point A to point A. Fig. 4.

4. Sew back seam and attach sole. Fig. 5.

5. Stuff legs right up to the top. Stitch openings closed.

6. Stuff body up to approximately 12 mm (½'') from neck opening. After the head is stitched to the body, the 'neck' will be loose and floppy. Fig. 6.

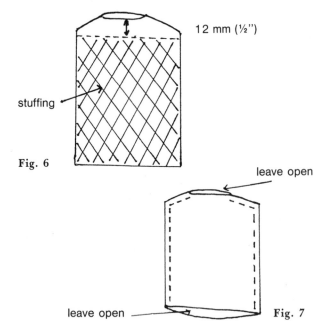

stuffing

12 mm (½")

Fig. 6

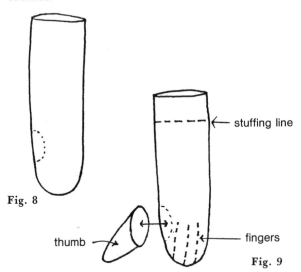

leave open

leave open

Fig. 7

Outer T-shirt fabric body

7. Cut out all pattern pieces in T-shirt fabric—outer body, legs, arms and shoulder plates (back and front).

8. Sew legs in the same way as those in calico. Sew up body, leaving neck and lower portion open. Fig. 7.

9. Sew up arms. Fig. 8.

10. Stuff arms to stuffing line. Sew up thumbs, stuff and attach to hands. Fig. 9.

11. Using strong thread, sew in fingers with a running stitch. See Fig. 9. Fists can be made with a few tacking stitches.

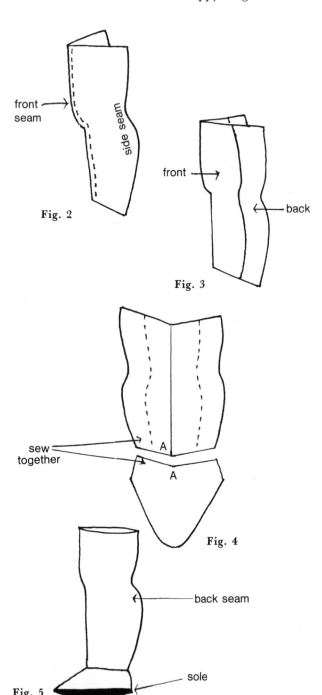

front seam

side seam

Fig. 2

front

back

Fig. 3

sew together

A

A

Fig. 4

back seam

sole

Fig. 5

Fig. 8

stuffing line

thumb

fingers

Fig. 9

12. Pull T-shirt body over stuffed calico body (in the same way as one would pull on a pair of socks) and sew up bottom section by hand. Fig. 10.

13. Insert stuffed calico legs into T-shirt legs. Fig. 11. Stitch toes in the same way as fingers.

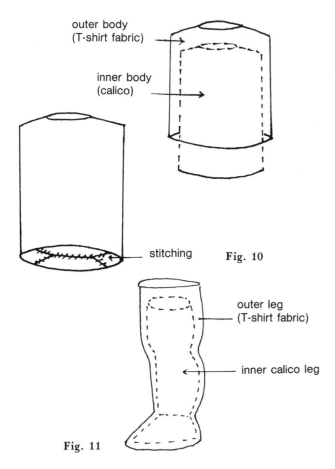

Fig. 10

Fig. 11

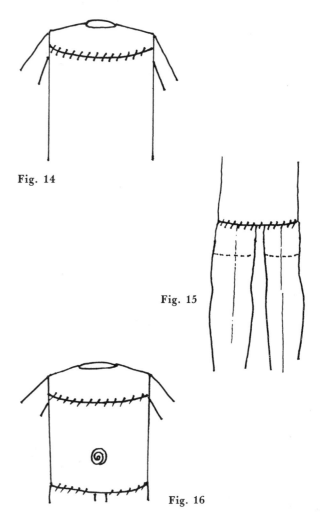

Fig. 14

Fig. 15

Fig. 16

14. Sew arms to shoulders. Fig. 12.

15. Sew back and front shoulder plates together. Fig. 13.

16. Place shoulder plates over top of body to hide stitching of the upper arms. Fig. 14. Turn a narrow hem and sew neatly by hand to the body.

17. Turn a narrow hem at top of legs and sew on to body. Fig. 15.

18. To make the navel, cut a strip of T-shirt fabric approximately 2.5 cm × 10 cm (1'' × 4''). Sew into a tube, roll into a coil and secure to body. Fig. 16.

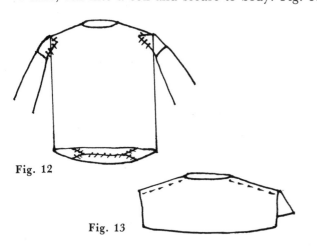

Fig. 12

Fig. 13

Painting the head

Materials required
paints (oils or acrylics) in pale flesh, coral, deep coral, light brown, dark brown and black
colourless varnish
fine sandpaper
brushes

1. Paint a pale flesh colour over the entire face. Add coral blush to the cheeks while the flesh paint is still wet. This allows the blush to blend in better.

2. Paint the mouth with a deep coral colour and place dots at nostrils. The mouth has no upper indentation, like the Käthe Kruse Doll XII.

3. The eyes are closed to represent a sleeping baby. Follow Fig. 17 to paint sleeping eyes and the contours of the mouth.

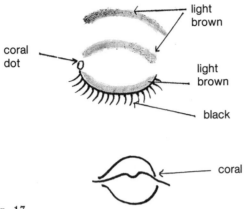

Fig. 17

PATTERNS FOR KÄTHE KRUSE TRÄUMERCHEN

Note: Enlarge all patterns to correct size by photocopying at 200%, *OR* enlarge by the grid method at 1 cm = 2 cm (½'' = 1'').

Seam allowance of 1 cm (⅜'') is included on all pattern pieces.

The head must be painted *before* it is attached to the body.

4. Paint the hair using a *dry* brush dipped lightly into brown paint. Brush onto head using light strokes to create the look of natural hair. Allow to dry. Fig. 18.

Fig. 18

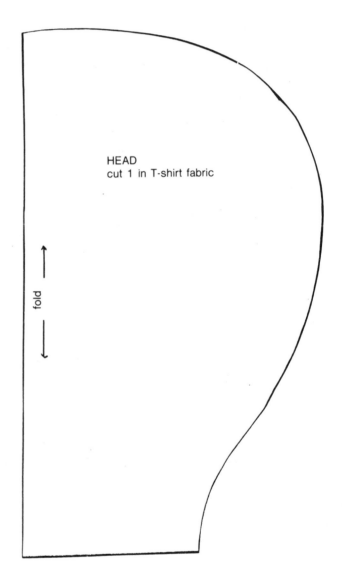

HEAD
cut 1 in T-shirt fabric

fold

5. When completely dry the painted areas might be rough to the touch. If this is so, sand gently with fine sandpaper until the desired smoothness is achieved.
6. Varnish the entire head with two coats of quick drying varnish. Put aside to dry.
7. Finally, place the neck neatly into the body opening and sew on firmly by hand. Alternatively, attach the head to the body using craft glue. Both methods are acceptable. Fig. 19.

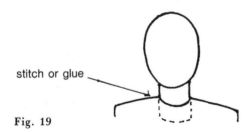

Fig. 19

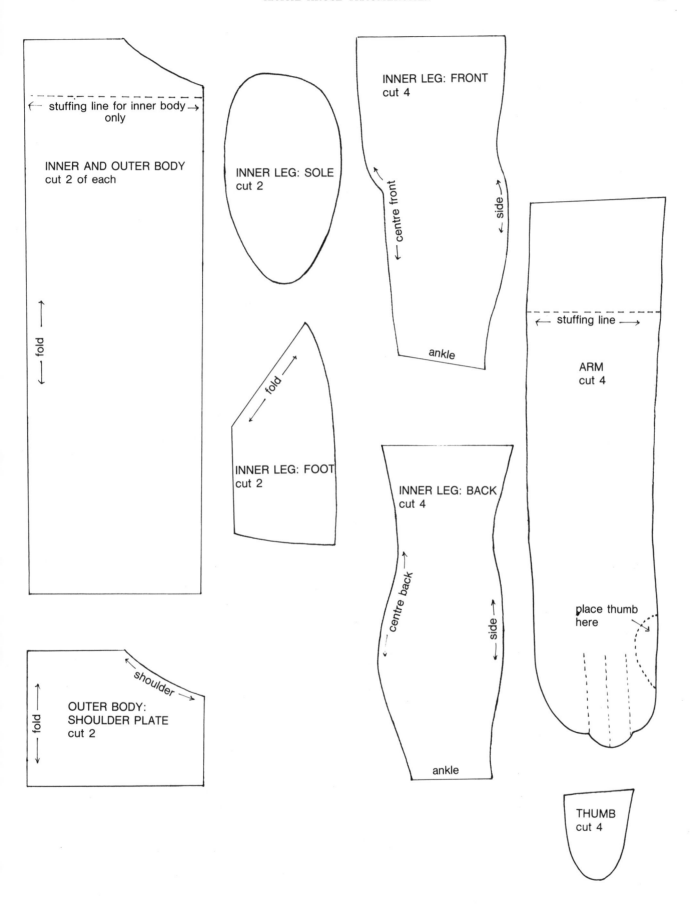

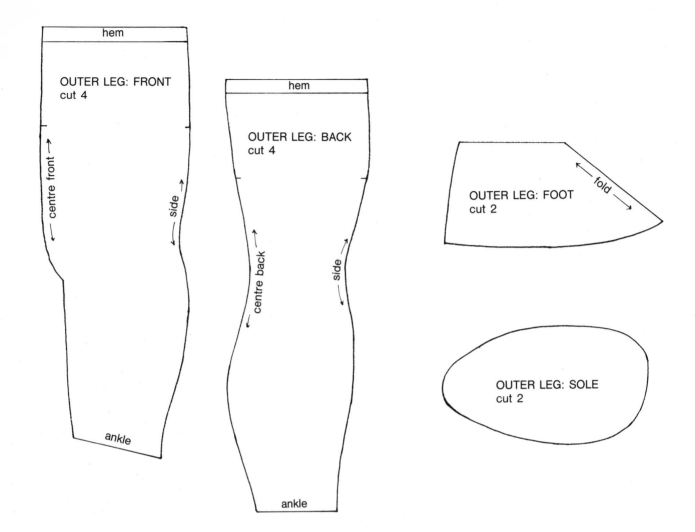

4 Dean's Rag Book Dolls

Illustrated on page 35

DEAN'S RAG BOOK DOLLS

This series was introduced by Dean & Son Ltd and Dean's Rag Book Co. Ltd, both of London, as far back as 1840. (The latter company had an established history of printing and publishing books designed in the shape of a doll.)

The faces of these dolls were of special significance, showing an interesting use of colour. The entire doll, including the head, was soft and suitable for children.

Felt was used in the manufacture of some of their models, originally felt made from beaver or rabbit fur and later from wool waste. It was considered a suitable medium since it could be steamed into shape, was hard wearing and was available in a variety of brilliant colours.

The Dean Group continues to produce good quality dolls in national costumes.

The instructions in this chapter are for the Dean's Rag Book Skater doll, which appears dressed in a green velvet costume with fur trim in the photograph on page 35. She is a copy of an original. The other three dolls in the photograph are my own designs using the characteristics of Dean's Rag Book dolls.

Making the head

Materials required
doll's head 28 cm (11'') circumference
piece T-shirt fabric large enough to fit over doll's face
rubber bands
paint brushes
0.5 m (½ yd) velvet (preferably old)
stuffing
turpentine
craft glue
Glad Wrap or similar
oil paints—flesh, white, black, blue, coral, Indian red
    (acrylics can be used to save drying time)
fabric stiffener or PVA woodworking glue
quick-drying artist's varnish

white fur fabric
mohair (available from any doll supplies store)

1. This doll has a soft stuffed head, only the face being moulded, in the form of a mask. To make the mask, soak the piece of T-shirt fabric in fabric stiffener and place it over the face of the doll's head. Smooth out all the bumps and wrinkles, pressing the material well into all the contours of the face. Secure fabric in position with rubber bands, taking care they do not distort the face. Allow to dry. Remove the mask from the head and cut away the excess fabric, beginning at the front of the ears. Figs 1 and 2.

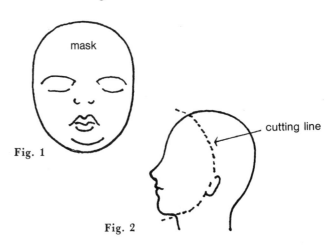

mask

Fig. 1

cutting line

Fig. 2

Painting the face mask

2. Place a layer of Glad Wrap over the doll's head and replace the mask. This gives you a firm foundation on which to work. Study the colour photograph on page 00 before you begin. It should help in painting the face.
3. Paint the entire face mask with a flesh coloured oil paint. Apply blush to the cheeks—a coral shade would be the best choice. Paint in the eyes following the contours of the eye area. See Fig. 3 for directions.
4. Paint the eyebrows with a single stroke in Indian red and the mouth in a coral shade. Allow to dry completely.
5. Cover with two coats of quick drying artist's gloss varnish. Allow to dry.

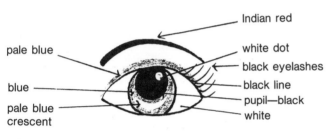

Fig. 3

6. Glue a few small pieces of mohair to the forehead of the mask. See Fig. 4.

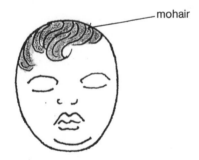

Fig. 4

Bonnet (back of head)

7. Cut out the three bonnet pattern pieces on page 00 from velvet fabric. Right sides facing, sew the two brim pieces together, on the outside edge only. Turn the material right side out. Fig. 4.
8. Pin the centre of the brim, marked A, to the centre of the mask forehead. Sew on by hand or machine. Fig. 5. Sew the short ends of the third piece (the head side) together to form a tube. Fig. 6.
9. Place the mask and brim inside one end of the tube, facing inwards. Sew together where indicated, by hand or machine. Make sure the seam is under the chin. Fig. 7.

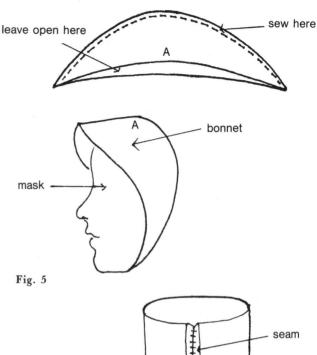

Fig. 5

Fig. 6

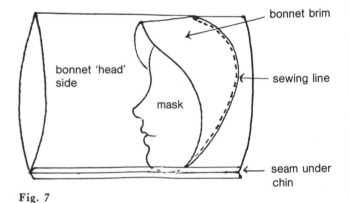

Fig. 7

10. Turn the tube right side out as you pull it over to the back of the head, freeing the brim. Fig. 8.

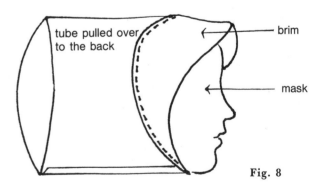

Fig. 8

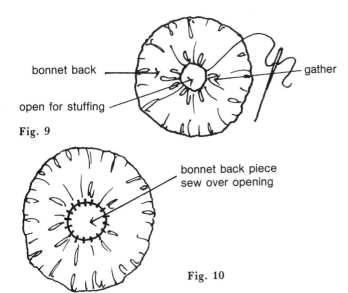

bonnet back ——— gather

open for stuffing

Fig. 9

bonnet back piece
sew over opening

Fig. 10

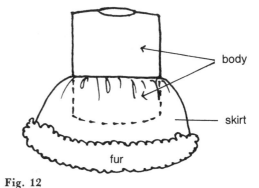

body

skirt

fur

Fig. 12

11. Using strong thread, sew a 2.5 cm (1'') hem around the open end of the tube and put a running stitch all around the opening. Pull the thread to gather the back of the head. Fig. 9.

12. Stuff the head firmly, then pull the thread up as tightly as possible to gather the fabric. Sew the two bonnet back pieces together, leaving a small opening, and turn inside out. Turn in the edges of the opening, and sew neatly to the back of the head by hand. Fig. 10.

13. Cut a narrow strip of fur fabric and sew to bonnet by hand along the brim seam line. Check the position in the colour photograph on page 35.

Body

14. Cut body pieces from velvet and sew together. Leave neck and bottom of body open. Fig. 11.

15. Cut skirt from velvet. Sew into a tube, make a narrow hem at the top and gather to fit body. Stitch neatly into position by hand. Make a narrow hem and stitch a band of fur fabric around hemline. Fig. 12.

16. Stuff the body in the usual way and sew up the bottom opening.

Arms and legs

17. Cut arms and legs from velvet, sew up and stuff. Make a narrow hem at the top of each arm and leg and sew neatly to the body. Using strong thread sew a tight band around each wrist and ankle to make hands and feet. Pin head to body and sew on neatly by hand. Figs 13 and 14.

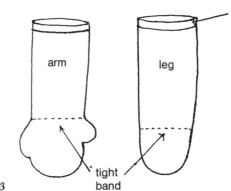

arm

leg

Fig. 13

tight
band

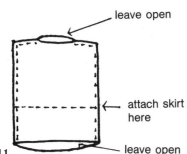

leave open

attach skirt
here

leave open

Fig. 11

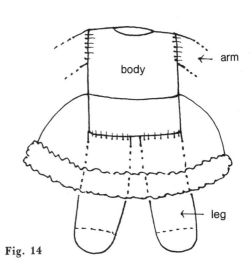

body

arm

leg

Fig. 14

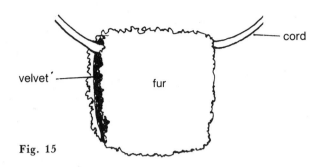

Fig. 15

Muff

18. Cut two pieces for the muff, one in fur and the other in velvet. Stitch long sides together. Turn inside out and seam short ends into a tube. Run a length of cord through the muff and hang it around the doll's neck. Fig. 15.

PATTERNS FOR DEAN'S RAG BOOK DOLLS

Note: Enlarge all patterns to correct size by photocopying at 200%, *OR* enlarge by the grid method at 1 cm = 2 cm (½" = 1").

Seam allowance of 1 cm (⅜") is included on all pattern pieces.

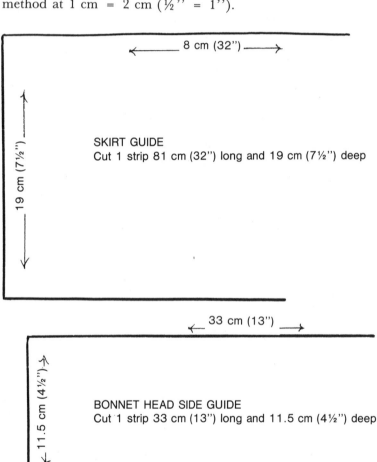

← 8 cm (32") →

19 cm (7½")

SKIRT GUIDE
Cut 1 strip 81 cm (32") long and 19 cm (7½") deep

← 33 cm (13") →

11.5 cm (4½")

BONNET HEAD SIDE GUIDE
Cut 1 strip 33 cm (13") long and 11.5 cm (4½") deep

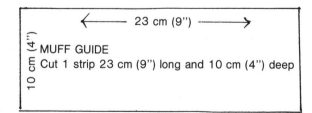

← 23 cm (9") →

10 cm (4")

MUFF GUIDE
Cut 1 strip 23 cm (9") long and 10 cm (4") deep

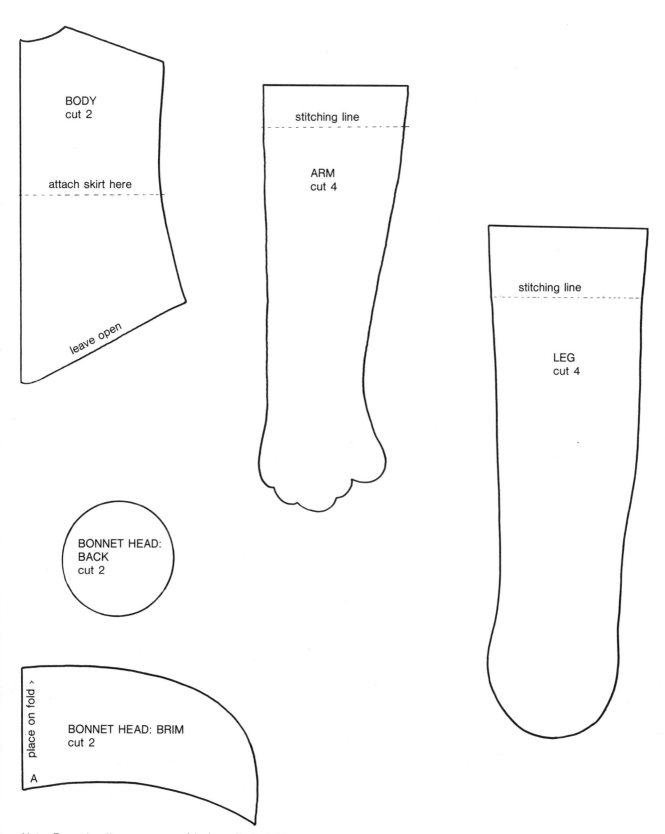

BODY
cut 2

attach skirt here

leave open

ARM
cut 4

stitching line

LEG
cut 4

stitching line

BONNET HEAD:
BACK
cut 2

place on fold >

BONNET HEAD: BRIM
cut 2

A

Note: Bonnet patterns may need to be adjusted if head circumference differs from the suggested 28 cm (11').

5 Nora Wellings Dolls

Illustrated on page 36

NORAH WELLINGS

Very little is known of the private life of Norah Wellings as few records remain. Her talents as a dollmaker are, however, clearly in evidence whenever her creations can be found.

Born in Arleston, England, in 1893, she began her career as a designer with the Chad Valley Company. In 1926, in association with her brother Leonard, she established her own dollmaking factory in nearby Wellington. Following successes in the early 1930s she was able to employ skilled workers, later moving to new and larger premises in an old chapel. With the purchase of the adjacent house and property, she had the use of a large garden and orchard which afforded pleasant surroundings for both her workers and visitors.

Most of her dolls were made of soft materials, predominantly velveteen, velour and cottons. She produced 'nationality' dolls which included Buckingham Palace Guards, South Sea Islanders and Canadian Mounties which were sold as souvenirs. Sailor dolls which had the name of a ship or port on the hatband were sold on ocean-going vessels of the Cunard Line. In a similar way, the Canadian Pacific Railway put her dolls up for sale in selected hotels as a reminder of a pleasant holiday.

On occasions she made special dolls for special people, the most famous being the gift of 'Cora', a model with glass eyes, moveable limbs and a felt face, to HM Queen Mary in 1927. In later years specials were made for and presented to members of the British Royal Family, notably to King George VI and Queen Elizabeth (now the Queen Mother) and their daughters Princess Elizabeth (now Queen Elizabeth II) and Margaret.

A great many models in a variety of designs were produced during the years that followed. It is worth noting that her collection of black dolls enjoyed considerable success. Unusually lifelike, both features and costumes were authentic—they were not simply white dolls painted black.

When her brother died in 1959, Norah Wellings closed her factory and went into retirement. She died in 1975 at the age of 82.

South Sea Island Girl

Materials required
0.5 m (½ yd) calico for body
T-shirt fabric approx. 30 cm (12'') square for head
  piece
T-shirt fabric approx. 10 cm (4'') square
  for mask
Glad Wrap
craft glue
rubber bands
doll's head approx. 18.5 cm (7¼'') circumference
fabric stiffener or PVA woodworking glue
stuffing
acrylic paints (brown, white, black, red)
paint brushes
quick-drying varnish
raffia, approx. 25 g (1 oz)
small coloured beads
black mohair (natural) from doll craft supplies shops

Opposite: Reproduction Izannah Walker doll with head made of moulded papier-mâché covered by painted fabric (page 8)

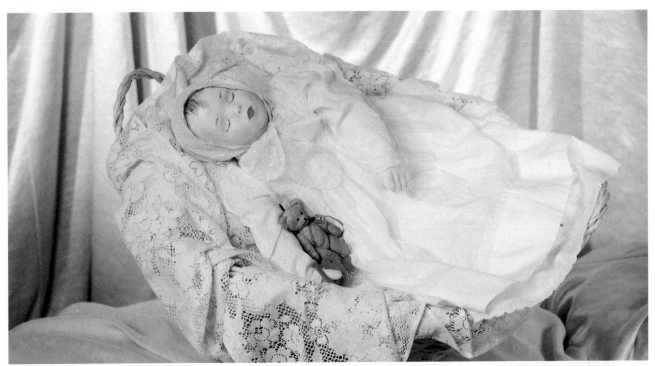

Reproduction Käthe Kruse Träumerchen, originally designed to teach baby care (page 21)

Opposite: Reproduction Käthe Kruse Doll XII showing the distinctive mouth shape with no depression in the upper lip (page 16)

Reproduction Dean's Rag Book dolls. The skater (dressed in green) is a copy of an original. The other dolls are modern interpretations (page 27)

Head

1. Soak piece of T-shirt fabric in fabric stiffener or PVA glue. Place Glad Wrap over doll's head. Remove T-shirt fabric from fabric stiffener (or PVA glue) and squeeze out excess. Place directly over the face of the doll's head. Press material into all corners and crevices. Smooth out with fingers so that there are no wrinkles. Secure with rubber bands and allow to dry.

When dry, remove fabric (mask) from head. It should be stiff to the touch. If not stiff enough, replace mask over doll's face and brush on more stiffener (PVA glue if this has been used initially) and put aside to dry. See Fig. 1.

2. Remove mask when dry and trim away any excess material from areas in front of the ears. See Fig. 2.

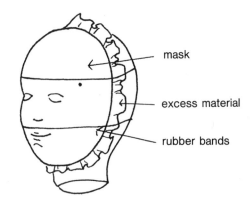

Fig. 1

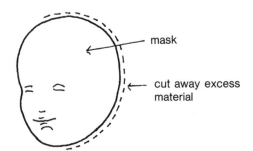

Fig. 2

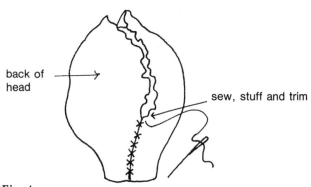

Fig. 3

3. Cut out head piece pattern in T-shirt fabric. Cover entire mask with craft glue and place the head piece directly over the mask. Ensure the material is pressed in to all corners and crevices. See Fig. 3.

4. To form the back of the head, begin by taking the excess material at the neck around to the back. Fold to form the shape of a neck and begin oversewing by hand. Stuff neck while sewing to form the correct shape. Trim material during the process of folding; sew and stuff while moving to the top of the head. Keep a critical eye on the results of sewing and stuffing to ensure that the correct shape of a head is finally achieved. See Fig. 4.

5. There should be one seam up the back of the head from the base of the neck to approximately ear level. Make two or more darts from the top of the head to meet the vertical back seam. Getting this right requires a great deal of patience. It should not be done in a hurry. After all, the head is the most important part of the doll. See Fig. 5.

Fig. 4

Reproduction Nora Wellings dolls—a sailor boy (page 41) and a South Sea Island girl (page 32)

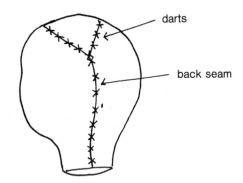

Fig. 5

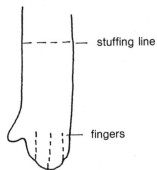

Fig. 8

Body

6. Using calico, cut out body pieces (arms and legs) from patterns. Sew body pieces together, leaving neck open for stuffing, and stuff.

Legs

7. Pin leg piece at A to upper foot at A. Pin B to B in a similar manner. Sew this seam, then sew back leg seam and attach soles.

8. Stuff legs to the stuffing line and sew across. Sew and stuff arms to stuffing line and sew across. Use a needle and strong thread to sew the fingers. See Figs 6, 7 and 8.

9. Place neck of head into neck opening of the body and hand sew into place. Fig. 9.

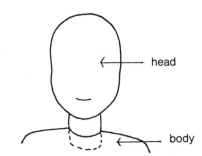

Fig. 9

10. Make narrow hems at the open ends of the arms and legs and sew by hand to the body. Fig. 10.

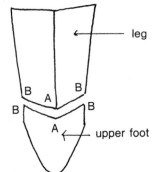

Fig. 6

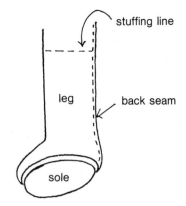

Fig. 7

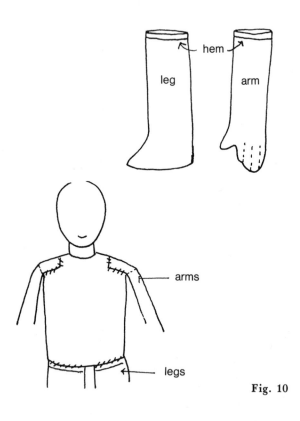

Fig. 10

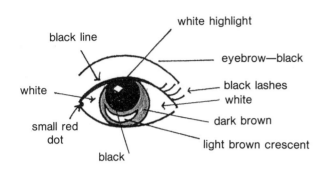

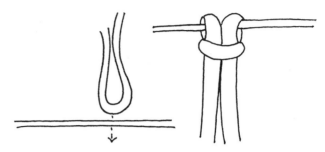

Fig. 12

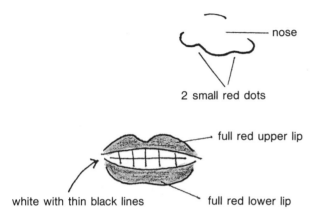

Fig. 11

Painting
10. Paint the entire doll with brown paint. Paint features using the diagram in Figure 11; check also the colour photograph on page 36. When dry, apply two coats of quick-drying varnish.

Hair
11. Using your fingers, carefully tease out a piece of black mohair so that it is sufficient to cover the entire top and back of the head. Glue to head with craft glue.

Skirt
12. Lay a strand of raffia on a flat surface such as a table. Cut several 25 cm (10'') lengths of raffia, fold each in half and fix to 'waist-band'. See Fig. 12. Continue this process until the skirt is large enough to fit the waist of the doll.

Bodice
13. Wrap lengths of raffia around the doll's chest and secure with glue. Decorate with necklaces, bangles and earrings, using coloured beads. See photograph on page 36.

PATTERNS FOR NORA WELLINGS SOUTH SEA ISLAND GIRL

Note: Enlarge all patterns to correct size by photocopying at 200%, *OR* enlarge by the grid method at 1 cm = 2 cm (½'' = 1'').

Seam allowance of 1 cm (⅜'') is included on all pattern pieces.

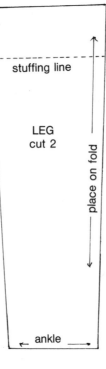

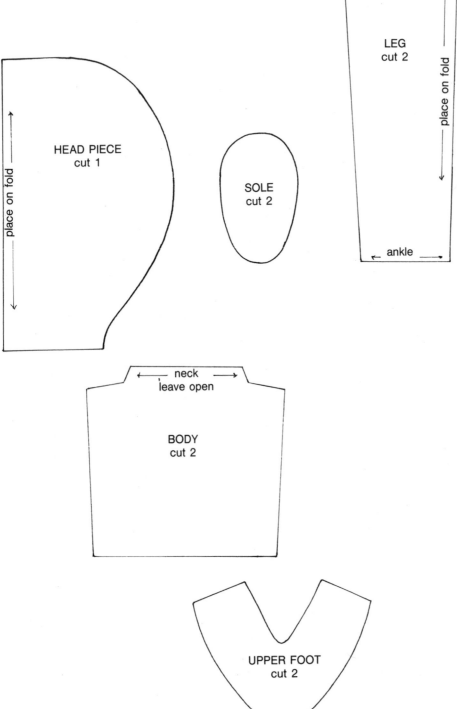

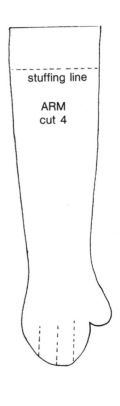

Sailor Boy

Materials required

small doll's head, approx. 18.5 cm (7¼'')
    circumference
fabric stiffener or PVA woodworking glue
craft glue
white T-shirt fabric approximately 30 cm (12'') square
    for head piece
white T-shirt fabric 10 cm (4'') square for mask
0.25 m (¼ yd) navy blue velveteen for body
black felt 10 cm (4'') square
white cotton fabric 30 cm (12'') square
blue bias binding
black ribbon 20 cm (8'') long, 1 cm (½'') wide
acrylic paints (flesh, white, black, blue, red, coral,
    brown)
paint brushes
quick-drying varnish
stuffing
Glad Wrap
0.25 m (¼ yd) white cotton fabric for hat and shirt
    front and back

Head

1. To fashion the head follow the instructions on pages 37–38 for the South Sea Island Girl except for the hair, which will be painted on in brown. The same doll's head can be used as a base.

Body

2. Cut out body, legs and arms in blue velveteen following enlarged patterns from page 44. Cut out shirt front and back in white cotton. Pin shirt front to front body piece and tack in place. Place bias binding around the V and sew on by hand or machine. See Fig. 1.

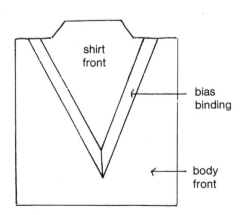

Fig. 1

3. Pin and tack shirt back body piece and trim with bias binding to match front. See Fig. 2.

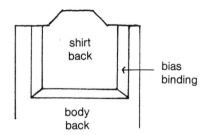

Fig. 2

4. Put back and front body pieces together, right sides facing, and sew up, leaving neck open for stuffing. Stuff firmly without lumps and put aside. Fig. 3.

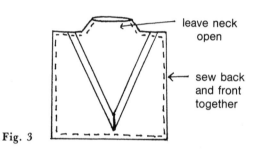

Fig. 3

Legs

5. Place leg pieces together, right sides facing. Sew side seams, leaving tops and bottoms open. Fig. 4.

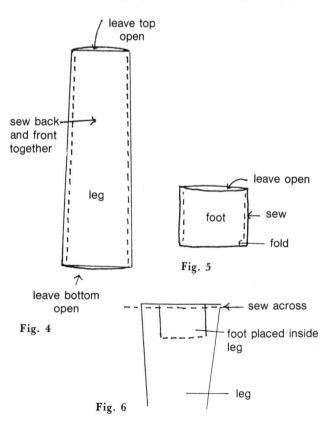

Fig. 4

Fig. 5

Fig. 6

6. Cut out two foot pieces from black felt following the pattern. Fold each foot piece in half, sew side seams and turn inside out. Insert folded edge of foot piece into bottom of leg and sew across. See Fig. 5.

7. Turn leg inside out and stuff to stuffing line. Fig. 6. Stuff foot lightly and stitch closed neatly.

8. Turn a narrow hem at top of leg and attach to body with neat stitches. See Fig. 7.

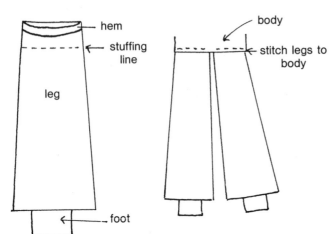

Fig. 7

Arms

9. Cut out hands in white cotton following pattern. Sew up, leaving wrists open, and turn right side out. Stuff sparingly and stitch lines through from front to back to form fingers, either by machine or hand.

Sew up back seam of arms, leaving top and bottom sections open.

10. Insert hand into wrist opening and sew across. See Fig. 8. Turn arm right side out, stuff to stuffing line and sew across. See Fig. 9.

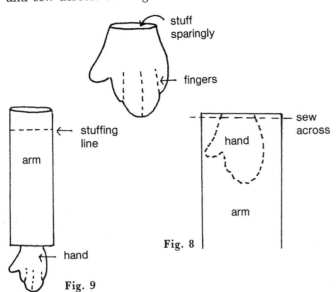

Fig. 8

Fig. 9

11. Make a narrow hem at the top opening of the arm and attach to shoulder by hand with neat stitches. See Fig. 10.

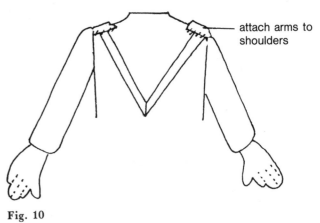

Fig. 10

Painting

12. Paint head and hands in flesh colour. Paint features following Fig. 11 and photograph on page 36.

Paint hair in dark brown, using a dry brush and light strokes around forehead and ears.

Apply two coats quick-drying varnish.

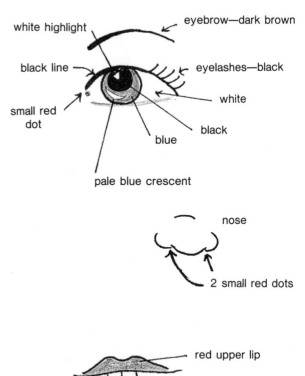

Fig. 11

Hat

13. Cut one lower crown and one upper crown in white cotton and one hat band, following the patterns on page 44. Cut notches around inside of lower crown. Sew hat band to notched area and cut away excess material. Fig. 12.

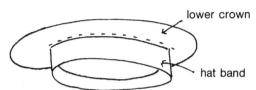

Fig. 12

14. Attach lower crown to upper crown, right sides facing, and turn right side out. See Fig. 13.

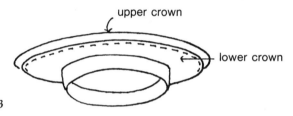

Fig. 13

15. Turn a narrow hem on the band and sew by hand. See Fig. 14.

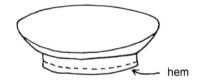

Fig. 14

16. Sew strip of bias binding around the band by hand. See Fig. 15.

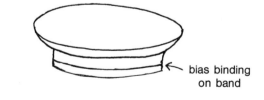

Fig. 15

17. Cut a 5 cm (2'') length of ribbon, fold at angle and stitch to side of hat band. See Fig. 16. Fold remaining length of ribbon and stitch to bottom of V section on shirt. See Fig. 16.

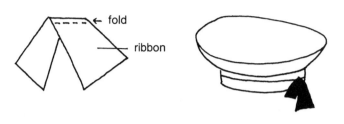

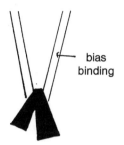

Fig. 16

18. You could letter the name of a naval vessel on the bias binding around the hat, as in the photograph on page 36.

PATTERNS FOR NORA WELLINGS SAILOR BOY

Note: Enlarge all patterns to correct size by photocopying at 200%, *OR* enlarge by the grid method at 1 cm = 2 cm (½'' = 1'').

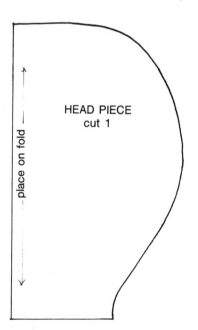

HEAD PIECE
cut 1

place on fold

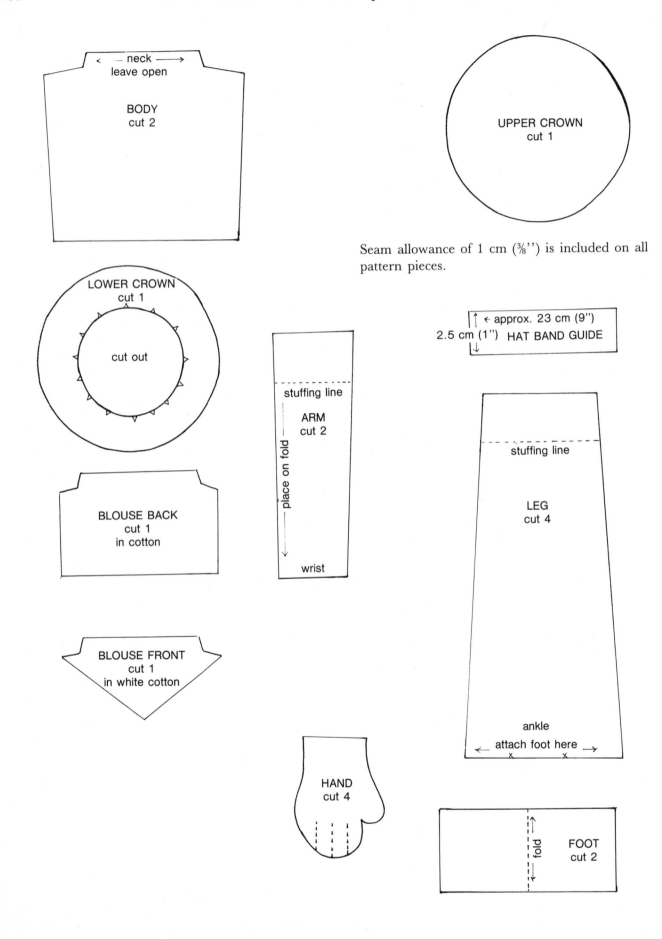

Seam allowance of 1 cm (⅜'') is included on all pattern pieces.

6 Papier-Mâché Baby

Illustrated on page 53

PAPIER-MÂCHÉ

Chapters 6, 7 and 8 deal with making dolls from an antique material rather than making antique dolls.

Papier-mâché literally means 'chewed paper'. It was introduced to doll making around the 1830s, though there is some evidence to suggest its commercial use in the late seventeenth and early eighteenth centuries to make dolls.

Papier-mâché is basically paper pulp mixed with water, to which is added fillers such as flour, meal, whiting or chalk and a binder such as glue or starch. Repellants were added occasionally to keep the finished product away from the depredations of rodents, and sweet smelling deodorisers to remove the odours resulting from such ingredients as animal glue.

Papier-mâché proved a popular medium for dollmaking, being an inexpensive product which was an obvious prerequisite for the success of any plan to manufacture and sell in large numbers.

Old records reveal that doll factories were often located near paper mills for easy access to the paper pulp. This led to their concentration in specific areas of the United Kingdom, the United States, Germany and, to a limited extent, France.

The early dollmakers found papier-mâché more satisfactory than most other mediums existing at the time. It was lighter and easier to handle, did not crack or crumble with normal handling and the drying process did not require the use of an oven. It responded well to the variety of finishes, such as wax and other lacquers, available at the time.

Modern dollmakers can make their own papier-mâché at home with a minimum of fuss but most will probably settle for the two commercially available sorts from craft shops. The first type, in powder form, is mixed with water to form a dough-like substance. It's a bit messy to work with but when dry is strong and hard to break. The second type, introduced fairly recently, comes in ready-to-use blocks. Small portions can be rolled out as required with a rolling pin. This type is recommended for small dolls where emphasis on detail is important.

Materials required
commercial mould set for a baby doll; can be any size but must include moulds for body, head, arms and legs
papier-mâché in block form or powder
acrylic paints (flesh, blue, brown, white, black, coral)
paint brushes
quick-drying varnish
fine sandpaper
craft glue
rubber bands
Vaseline
small quantity natural mohair
hat elastic
long toymaker's needle (from haberdashery store)
rolling pin

Body
1. If you choose to make a small doll, papier-mâché in block form is probably easier to handle. Roll out to a thickness of 4 mm (⅛'') with a rolling pin. Use powdered papier-mâché for a larger doll, prepared according to the instructions on the packet and being careful not to use too much water. Stand for approximately 15 minutes before use.
2. Apply coatings of Vaseline to the inner surface of all moulds. Press papier-mâché gently into each of the moulds and allow to dry thoroughly. If necessary, you

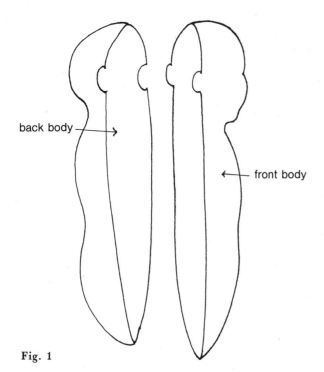

Fig. 1

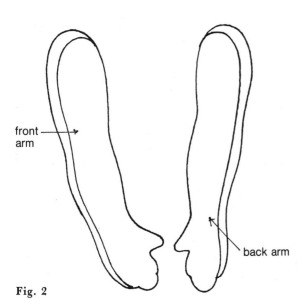

Fig. 2

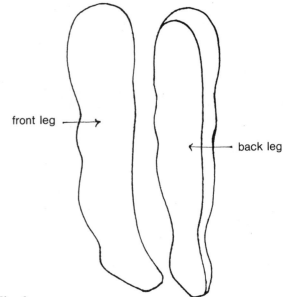

Fig. 3

can hasten the drying process by placing the moulds in a moderately hot oven. Leave moulds in oven until they cool off as they are liable to crack if removed suddenly from hot to cold temperatures. Check the oven frequently to ensure the papier-mâché is not overdone.

3. Papier-mâché has a tendency to shrink during the drying process which means that the pieces are fairly easily removed from the moulds.

4. Each doll section comes in two parts which should be glued together with craft glue. See Figs 1, 2 and 3. If necessary, trim any rough edges so that the pieces fit together snugly, apply glue liberally and secure with rubber bands until dry.

5. When the glue has dried apply more papier-mâché over all seam lines to conceal them and allow to dry. Using the toymaker's needle, pierce a hole through the upper part of each arm and leg and make matching holes in the upper and lower parts of the body. See Figs 4, 5 and 6.

6. Sandpaper each part gently, using a circular motion, until all surfaces are smooth to the touch.

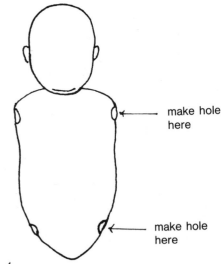

Fig. 4

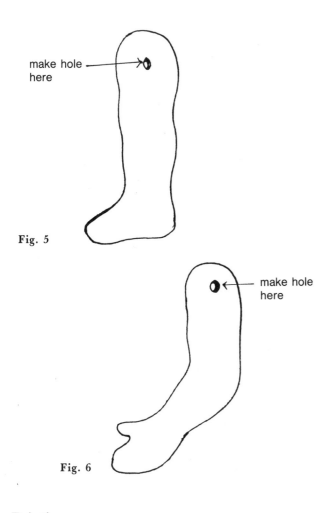

make hole here

Fig. 5

make hole here

Fig. 6

white highlight

eyebrow—brown

black

fine brown line

coral dot

thick black line

white

blue

pale blue crescent

nose

coral dots for nostrils

mouth coral

Fig. 7

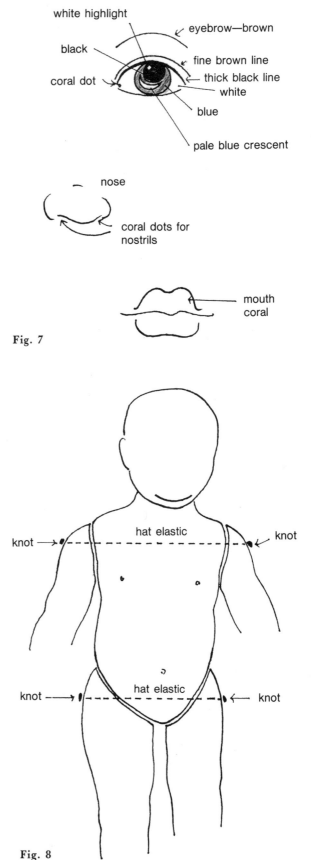

knot

hat elastic

knot

knot

hat elastic

knot

Fig. 8

Painting

7. Paint entire doll in flesh colour; while wet blush cheeks with coral. Dry thoroughly. Paint in features following suggestions in Fig. 7. Dry thoroughly and apply two or three coats of quick-drying varnish.

Hair

8. Use your fingers to gently tease out the natural mohair and apply it to the head with craft glue. A word of caution—use very little mohair for a realistic look, as most babies tend to be quite bald!

Putting doll together

9. Thread hat elastic through the toymaker's needle and make a large enough knot at the end to prevent the elastic slipping through the holes in the doll. Push needle through the hole in one arm, with the knot on the *outside* of the arm, through the body at shoulder level and out through the other arm. Pull elastic fairly tight and make a knot. The arms should be tight against the body but able to move freely. Do the same for the legs. See Fig. 7.

10. Dress the finished doll in appropriate clothing.

7 Papier-mâché Ladies

Illustrated on page 53

Materials required

commercial mould (the dolls described here were made using an early German lady doll by J.D. Kestner, head size approx. 21.5 cm (8½''), the complete mould including shoulder plate, arms and legs with boots

0.5 m (½ yd) calico for body

stuffing

papier-mâché in block form

Vaseline

acrylic paints (flesh, brown, black, white, coral, blue)

paint brushes

rolling pin

craft knife

rubber bands

quick-drying gloss varnish

craft glue

fine sandpaper

small piece natural mohair

1 bolt approx. 2.5 cm (1'') long

2 metal washers approx. 2.5 cm (1'') dia. to suit bolt

1 wing nut to suit bolt

2 circles felt, size similar to washers

1. Apply Vaseline to all mould pieces and put aside.

2. Working with small quantities, roll out papier-mâché to a thickness of approximately 4 mm (⅛''). Gently press, piece by piece, into the moulds, ensuring that all holes, corners and crevices are covered. Allow to dry.

The moulds can be placed in a slow oven to speed up the drying process if necessary. Check frequently to see that they are not overdone. Leave the moulds in the oven to cool off gradually as sudden removal from heat may result in cracks and irregularities. When completely dry the papier-mâché pieces should come away from the moulds quite easily.

3. You should have two head pieces (back and front), four arm pieces, four leg pieces and a shoulder plate. With a pair of scissors or other sharp-pointed instrument make four holes in the shoulder plate, one in each corner front and back. See Fig. 1.

4. Carefully trim pieces with a craft knife to ensure smooth-fitting seams. Join each piece to its corresponding piece using craft glue, holding them tightly together with a rubber band until the glue is completely dry. See Fig. 2.

5. Remove rubber bands and apply more papier-mâché over all seam lines and fill in any holes and crevices. When dry, sandpaper until smooth.

6. Cut away top of head with a craft knife. Fig. 3.

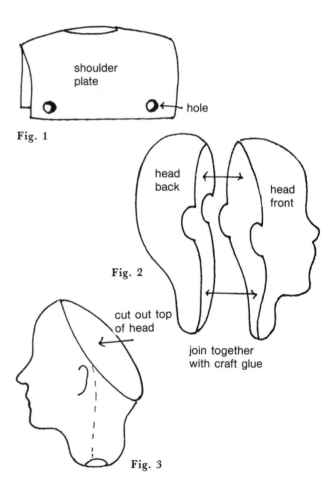

Fig. 1

shoulder plate

hole

head back

head front

Fig. 2

join together with craft glue

cut out top of head

Fig. 3

Painting

7. Paint all pieces in flesh. While wet, use a little coral to lightly blush cheeks and tops of hands. Paint in features following contours of face, using Fig. 4 as a guide.

8. Boots can be painted any colour you choose, but paint feet in flesh.

9. Finish with two or three coats of varnish. Leave to dry.

10. If you intend your doll to have hair, glue the mohair on at this point.

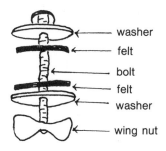

Fig. 5

followed by the wing nut. See Fig. 5 for correct assembly. The felt circles must be between the metal washers and the papier-mâché. Tighten wing nut firmly.

Completing the head

12. This is simply a method of covering the top head opening, at the same time providing a hat, cap, turban or other covering or headgear. Measure a length of fabric to fit around the head opening approximately 10 cm (4'') wide. The width depends on the type of covering you want. Cut and pin to fit. Sew fabric into a tube and glue to head. Any untidiness will be hidden by trimming later. Make a narrow hem at other end and run a gathering thread through. Gather and tighten while stuffing the head. Tighten securely when required head shape is achieved. Fig. 6.

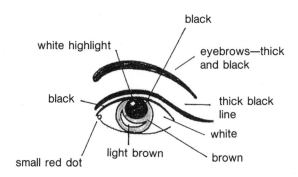

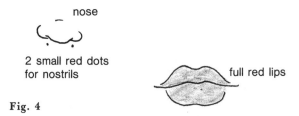

Fig. 4

Joining head to shoulder plate

11. Insert bolt down through top of head and shoulder plate, first fitting a felt circle and a metal washer. At the bottom end, place a felt circle and a metal washer

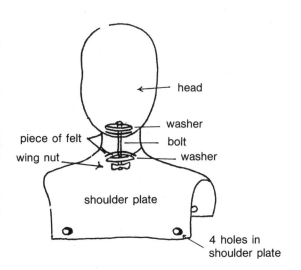

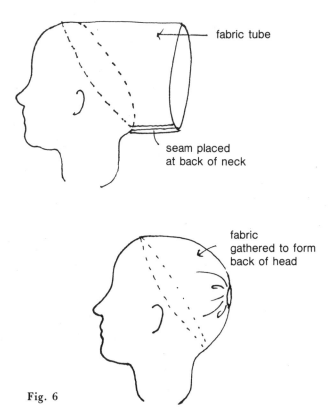

Fig. 6

Body

13. Cut out body pieces in calico. Sew darts and sew up seams leaving neck open for stuffing. Stuff firmly and close neck opening. Fig. 7.

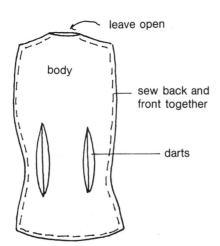

Fig. 7

Arms and legs

14. Sew up cloth arms and legs. Leave cloth legs wrong side out after sewing and place the papier-mâché legs inside with the seams at the back. Glue the cloth legs to the tops of the papier-mâché legs and bind tightly with strong thread. Reverse the cloth legs and stuff. Do the same for the arms. Fig. 8.

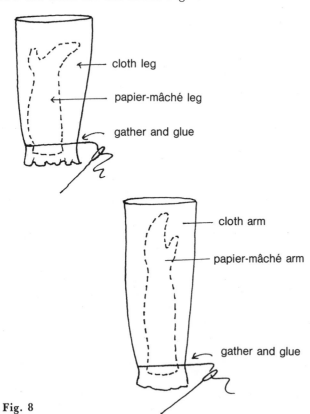

Fig. 8

15. Sew arms and legs to body. Fig. 9.

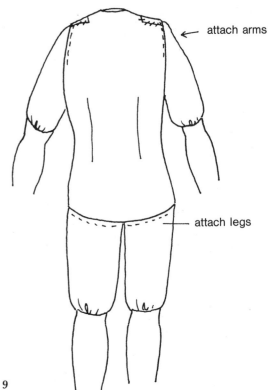

Fig. 9

Shoulder plate

16. Cut 4 strips of calico approximately 12 cm × 1 cm (5'' × ½''). Thread each strip into one of the holes in the shoulder plate. Place shoulder plate directly on to body. Secure by stitching fabric strips firmly to the body. Fig. 10.

17. Dress doll as ornately and flamboyantly as possible, using bright fabrics, beads, sequins, glitter and so on.

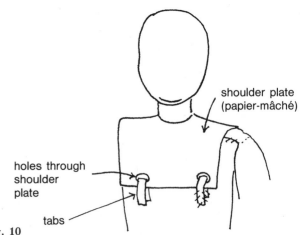

Fig. 10

PATTERNS FOR PAPIER-MÂCHÉ LADIES

Note: Enlarge all patterns to correct size by photocopying at 200%, *OR* enlarge by the grid method at 1 cm = 2 cm (½'' = 1'').

Seam allowance of 1 cm (⅜'') is included on all pattern pieces.

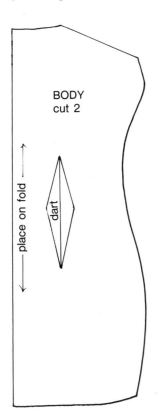

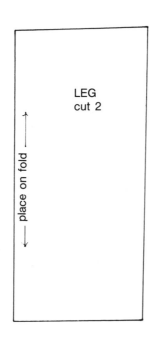

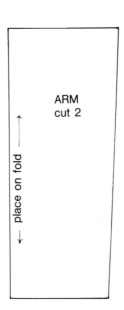

8 Papier-mâché Black Doll

Illustrated opposite

Materials required

commercial mould including head 28 cm (11'') in circumference, arms and legs, or homemade head mould
0.5 m (½ yd) calico for body
papier-mâché (both block and powder)
Vaseline
acrylic paints (brown, black, white, red)
craft glue
paint brushes
rubber bands
craft knife
fine sandpaper
rolling pin
quick-drying gloss varnish

Head

1. Apply Vaseline to the inside of the moulds. Put aside. Roll out small quantities of block papier-mâché to a thickness of approximately 4 mm (⅛''). Gently press, piece by piece, into the moulds, ensuring that all holes, corners and crevices are covered. Allow to dry, using the oven if necessary (see page 48).

2. Trim pieces carefully with a craft knife. Join back and front using craft glue. Secure with a rubber band until they have bonded completely.

3. Remove rubber band and apply more papier-mâché over all seam lines, filling in holes and crevices. When dry, sandpaper until smooth. Fig. 1.

4. Mix a small quantity of powdered papier-mâché with water in a bowl. Avoid a tacky solution. Allow to stand for approximately fifteen minutes, then apply thickly to doll's head, with a rough finish, for hair. See photograph opposite and Fig. 2.

5. Roll out a small quantity of block papier-mâché, approximately 5 cm (2'') long and 8 mm (¼'') thick. Form into an open loop and press into hair as a base for a ribbon. Fig. 2. Allow to dry.

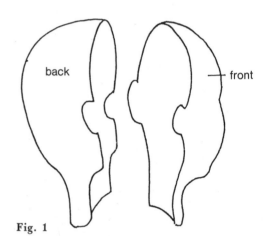

back   front

Fig. 1

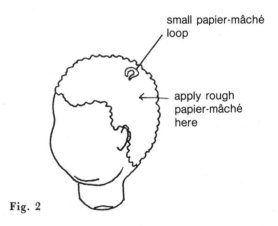

small papier-mâché loop

apply rough papier-mâché here

Fig. 2

Body

6. Cut out body pieces in calico. Sew up, leaving neck open for stuffing, and stuff. Fig. 3.

Papier-mâché arms and legs

7. If you are using a commercial mould with arms and legs follow the same procedure as for making the head. If moulds are not available it's quite easy to make arms and legs from papier-mâché if you have other arms and legs of appropriate size.

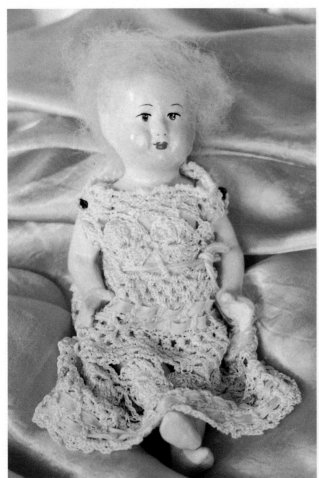

Above: Papier-mâché black doll (opposite)

Above left: Papier-mâché baby (page 45)

MODERN DOLLS MADE FROM AN ANTIQUE MATERIAL

Papier-mâché ladies (page 48)

Reproduction Columbian doll, designed by Emma Adams in the late nineteenth century (page 64)

Reproduction Martha Jenks Chase doll (page 68)

A modern version of the turn-of-the-century Lithographed doll, made with the aid of a colour photocopying machine (page 87)

Reproduction Steiff Clown doll, one of the many Steiff character dolls (page 78)

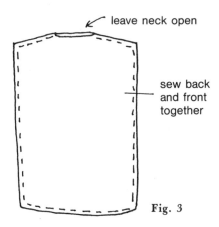

leave neck open

sew back
and front
together

Fig. 3

Apply Vaseline to the arms and legs, up to the elbows for the arms and up to the knees for the legs. Roll out block papier-mâché and apply directly to arms and legs, covering the surfaces entirely and joining smoothly. Allow to dry.

Do not place these pieces in an oven to dry as the inner doll components are liable to melt.

8. Using a craft knife cut papier-mâché into two sections. See Fig. 4. If you are unsure of your hand draw a light pencil line on the papier-mâché first.

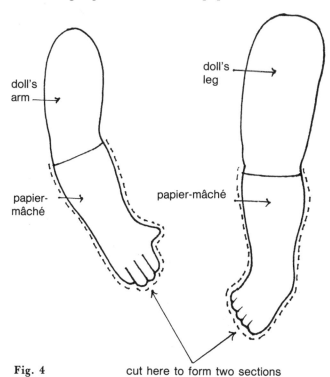

doll's
arm

doll's
leg

papier-
mâché

papier-mâché

Fig. 4   cut here to form two sections

9. Join back and front pieces together with craft glue and secure with rubber bands until dry. Remove rubber bands and cover all seam lines and any imperfections with more papier-mâché. When dry, smooth to a fine finish with sandpaper.

Painting

10. Paint all surfaces apart from the hair in dark brown. Paint in features following Fig. 5 and the photograph on page 53. Paint hair in black. When dry, apply two coats of quick-drying varnish.

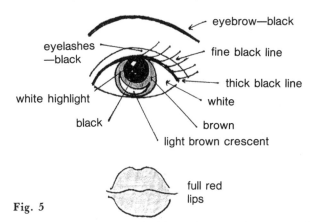

eyebrow—black

eyelashes
—black

fine black line

thick black line

white highlight

white

black

brown

light brown crescent

full red
lips

Fig. 5

11. Thread a length of ribbon through the loop in the hair and tie a bow.

Calico arms and legs

12. Cut out arms and legs in calico. Leave the cloth leg in the inside out position after sewing and place papier-mâché leg inside, with the seam at the back. Glue the cloth leg to the papier-mâché leg and bind tightly with strong thread. Reverse the cloth leg and stuff. Do the same for the other leg and arms. Fig. 6.

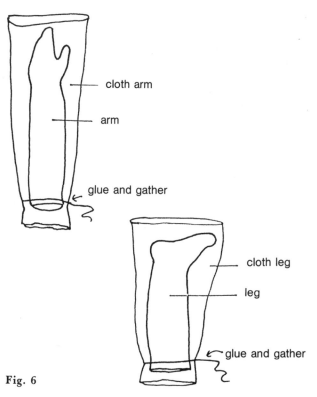

cloth arm

arm

glue and gather

cloth leg

leg

glue and gather

Fig. 6

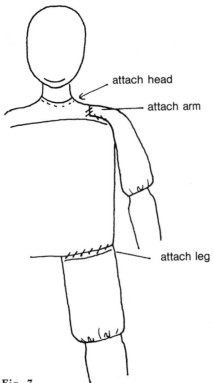

Fig. 7

13. Attach arms and legs to body. Fig. 7.

Attaching head to body
14. Insert neck into body opening. Gather fabric around neck if necessary and bond with craft glue or by sewing. Fig. 8.
15. Dress doll appropriately.

PATTERNS FOR PAPIER-MÂCHÉ BLACK DOLL

Note: Enlarge all patterns to correct size by photocopying at 200%, *OR* enlarge by the grid method at 1 cm = 2 cm (½'' = 1'').

Seam allowance of 1 cm (⅜'') is included on all pattern pieces.

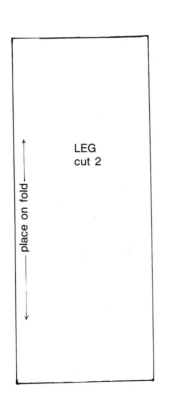

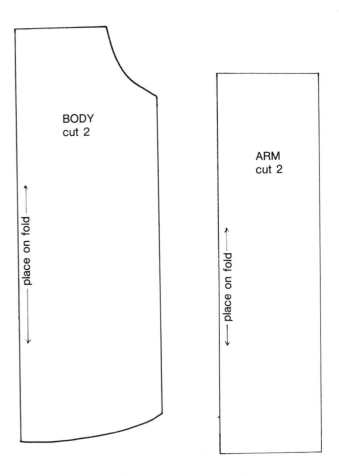

9 Lenci Doll

Illustrated on page 73

LENCI

In the early 1920s the 'Art Doll', a new concept in doll-making, was introduced. It was intended to be not only a toy for children but a fashion accessory for the young women of the day. In order to produce what would later be regarded as works of art, artists and sculptors were brought in to design heads and faces.

The best known of this group of dollmakers was the Italian company Lenci owned by Enrico Scavini. The company was named after his wife Elena's pet name. Lenci produced superb felt dolls with pressed felt faces, faces that were appealing since they were mostly of young children where there was ample scope for natural and varied expressions. The outfits were also designed professionally with emphasis on bright colours and floral designs.

Lenci later marketed a sporting series—these dolls were accompanied by a tennis racquet, golf clubs and other items relevant to a particular sport.

The most famous of all Lenci dolls is, perhaps, the one produced at the end of the 1920s which depicted the film star Rudolph Valentino and was targeted at his many female fans around the world.

Materials required

commercial or handmade head mould, 30 cm (12'') circumference
powdered papier-mâché
Vaseline
craft knife
rubber bands
fine sandpaper
0.5 m (½ yd) cream felt
acrylic paints (dark brown, white, black, blue, pink)
doll's wig to fit
paint brushes (fine)
powder blush makeup
craft glue
4 buttons
strong thread or twine
toymaker's needle
stuffing

Head

1. Follow the instructions given for making a head in papier-mâché on pages 8–10, with one exception—this head will be covered in felt, not T-shirt fabric.
2. Once the head is dry, cut out a square of felt large enough to cover it entirely back and front. Apply craft glue to the face, taking special care to cover areas such as the eyes, nose, mouth and behind the ears, while soaking the felt in boiling water. When the temperature has dropped enough for the felt to be comfortable to the touch, squeeze out excess water. Place felt directly over the face, using your fingers to press it into all crevices, holes and corners. If this is not done thoroughly, the correct contours of the face will not be achieved.
3. Cover the back of the head with craft glue. Extend the felt from the face area around to the back of the head. Bond the felt with the glue and sew up to follow the shape of the back of the head, trimming away extra felt. This should be done as neatly as possible but should any imperfections appear they will be covered by the wig.

Body, arms and legs

4. Cut out body, arms and legs in cream felt following enlarged patterns from page 62. Sew up centre seam of front body pieces. Sew up back seam of back body pieces. Fig. 1.
5. Join back and front, leaving neck open, and stuff. Fig. 2.

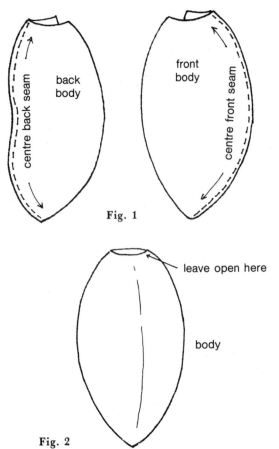

Fig. 1

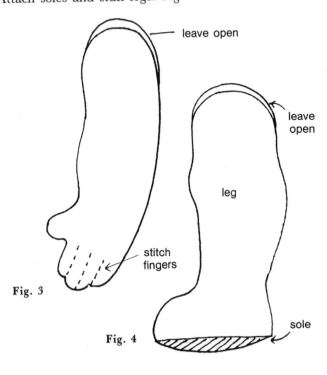

Fig. 2

Attaching arms and legs
8. With thread double insert toymaker's needle through body at shoulder level, bringing it out at the other side.

Pass needle through top of arm and through holes in button as shown in Fig. 5. Tie a knot and secure.

Complete stuffing and sew up arm. Do the same for the other arm. Pull thread or twine tightly and knot. Attach legs in the same manner. The arms and legs should be firm against the body but moveable. See Figs 5 and 6 for details.

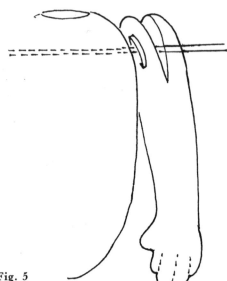

Fig. 5

6. Sew up arms, leaving top open for stuffing. Stuff. Sew fingers, stitching right through from front to back. Fig. 3.
7. Sew front and back seams of legs, leaving tops open. Attach soles and stuff legs. Fig. 4.

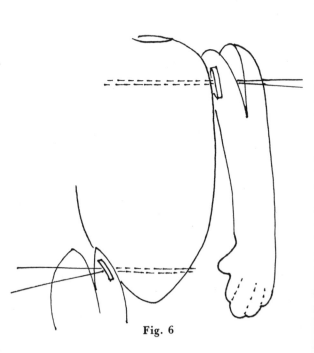

Fig. 3

Fig. 4

Fig. 6

Attaching head to body

9. Fit neck into body opening. Bond with craft glue or stitch together, gathering fabric if required. Fig. 7.

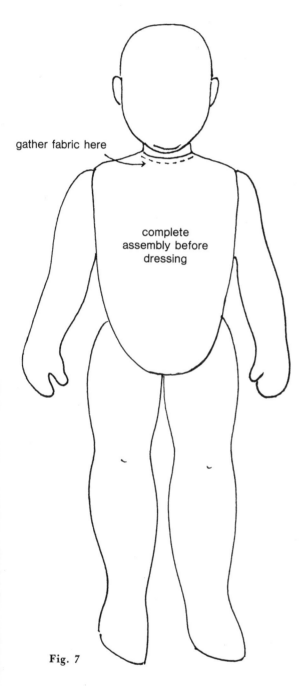

gather fabric here

complete
assembly before
dressing

Fig. 7

Painting the face

10. Since felt does not have a smooth surface texture, painting the face can sometimes be quite difficult. A fine paint brush makes the task a lot easier. Begin by painting the whites of the eyes. Outline eyes in dark brown followed by eyebrows in the same colour. Paint irises blue with a lighter blue crescent under black pupils. Place a small white dot at the upper corner of each pupil as a highlight.

Put a small pink dot at each nostril. Paint lips pink (most Lenci dolls had pink lips). Blush cheeks with powder makeup. When face is completely dry, glue on the wig. See Fig. 8 and photograph on page 73.

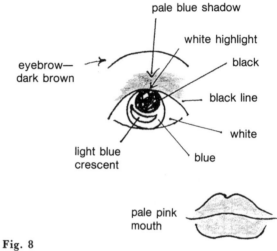

pale blue shadow

white highlight

eyebrow—
dark brown

black

black line

white

light blue
crescent

blue

pale pink
mouth

Fig. 8

Clothes

11. To dress the doll in authentic Lenci fashion you will need:

0.5 m (½ yd) red felt for dress and shoes
white felt for the collar
small pieces of coloured felt for flowers
white T-shirt fabric for socks
3 buttons and pinking shears

Follow enlarged patterns from page 63.

PATTERNS FOR LENCI DOLL

Note: Enlarge all patterns to correct size by photocopying at 200%, *OR* enlarge by the grid method at 1 cm = 2 cm (½'' = 1'').

Seam allowance of 1 cm (⅜'') is included on all pattern pieces.

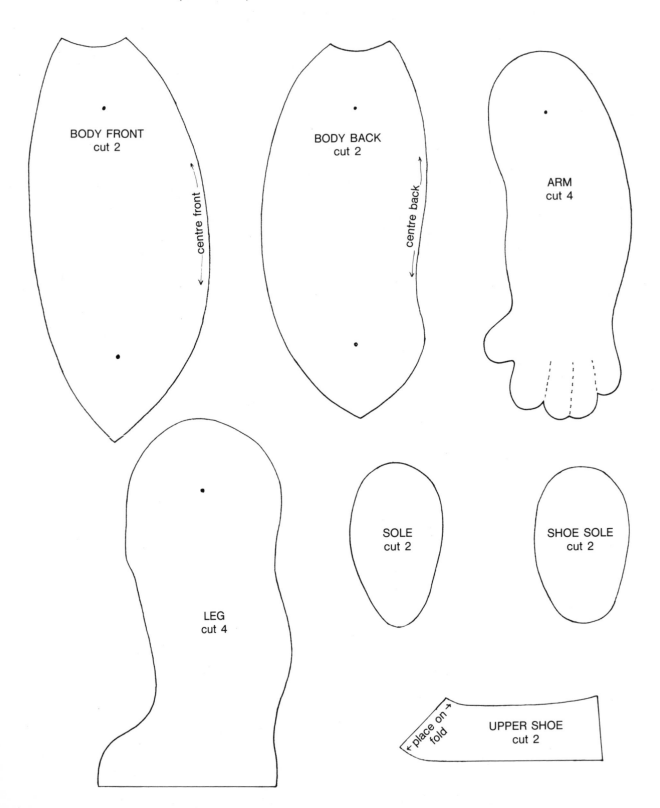

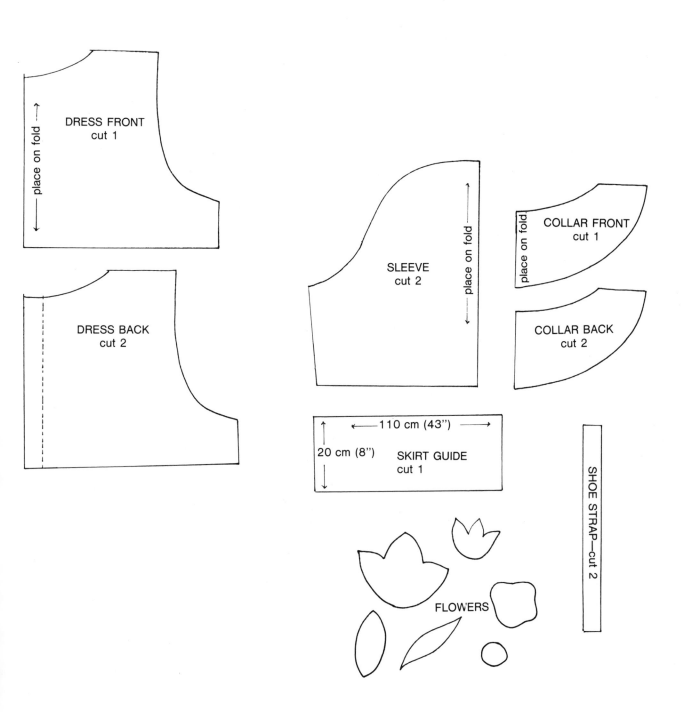

10 Columbian Doll

Illustrated on page 54

EMMA AND MARIETTA ADAMS

What is a rag doll? Not much really. Put together from old rags, quite literally from a 'rag bag', with wool, flax or cornsilk for hair, eyes from old shoe buttons and faces painted or embroidered. Cut out, stitched and stuffed with results depending entirely on the individual talents of the maker.

This, then, was the Columbian Doll, no more and no less—a doll which by an extraordinary set of circumstances gained unusual success during its early years in the late 1890s.

Credit for its origins must go to Miss Emma Adams. Born in New York in 1858, she was known initially for her portrait paintings, which later proved to be a tremendous asset. Encouraged by friends to make a doll, she did so in 1891 and on showing it to the well known department store Marshall Field & Co. she received an order for a limited number.

Considering that dollmaking might be a profitable business she was joined by her sister Marietta. They launched the doll commercially towards the end of the century after improving upon the construction of the body and the painting of the face. The two sisters worked well together, Emma painting the faces and Marietta designing the dresses.

In 1893 Emma's dolls were exhibited at the Columbia Exposition of the Chicago World Fair where a large number was sold. It was at this point that she named the doll 'Columbian'. Not long afterward the doll attracted the attention of a wealthy doll collector, a Mrs Horton of Boston, Massachusetts. Receiving a gift of a Columbian doll from Emma and Marietta, she added it to her international collection which she exhibited to raise funds for needy children around the world, travelling to Mexico, Alaska, India, the Philippines, Hong Kong, Singapore, China and Ceylon, visiting places like Suez and Palestine on the journey back to New York.

Emma Adams died in 1900 at the age of 42, and Marietta assumed the responsibility of the business though commercial artists were given the task of painting faces. It was a success until a fever epidemic in her family in 1911 forced her to discontinue the business, though records indicate that some dolls were made as late as 1924. Marietta died in 1944.

The American press described the Columbian dolls as 'Queens of Dolldom' with full credit going to their creators Emma and Marietta Adams.

Materials required

0.5 m (½ yd) calico
stick or dowel approx. 20 cm (8'') long × pencil thickness
stuffing
acrylic paints (black, white, coral, blue, brown, yellow, flesh)
quick-drying varnish
brushes

1. Cut out body pieces in calico.

2. Sew up the three darts at the neckline on both the back and front of the pattern. See Fig. 1.

3. Sew body together and turn right side out. Leave top open for stuffing. Commence stuffing firmly but without lumps. On reaching the halfway point, place stick or dowel inside body so that it reaches up into the neck area. See Fig. 2.

Complete stuffing and close by hand stitching.

4. Sew arms, turn right side out and stuff to stuffing line. Sew across at stuffing line. See Fig. 3. Sew fingers either by hand or machine.

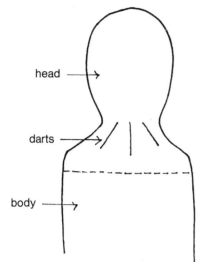

Fig. 1

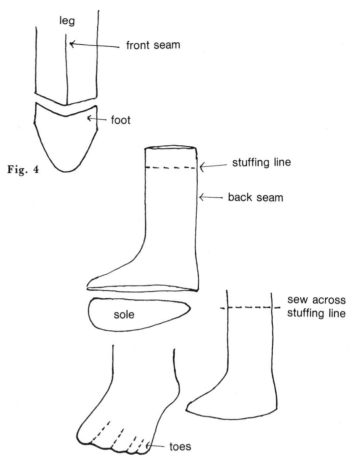

Fig. 4

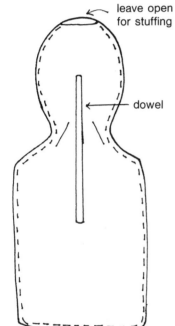

Fig. 2

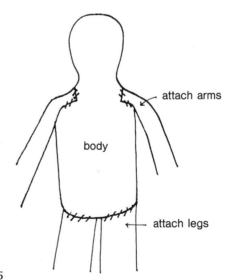

Fig. 5

5. Sew front leg seams and attach feet. Sew back leg seams and attach soles. Stuff to stuffing line and sew across. See Fig. 4.

6. Sew toes either by hand or machine. See Fig. 5.

7. Attach arms and legs to the body. See Fig. 6.

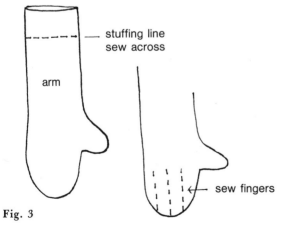

Fig. 3

Fig. 6

Painting

8. Apply a coat of flesh colour paint to entire head, arms and legs. (The entire body may be painted if you wish.) While wet, blush the cheeks with coral and blend colours carefully. Paint eyes, nose and mouth following the guide in Fig. 7. Paint hair in curls using yellow. See Fig. 7 also. Allow to dry.

Dress

9. Old-fashioned prints are ideal for this doll. I dressed mine in a gathered gingham pinafore with ties over the shoulders, a lace-trimmed blouse and a pretty bonnet.

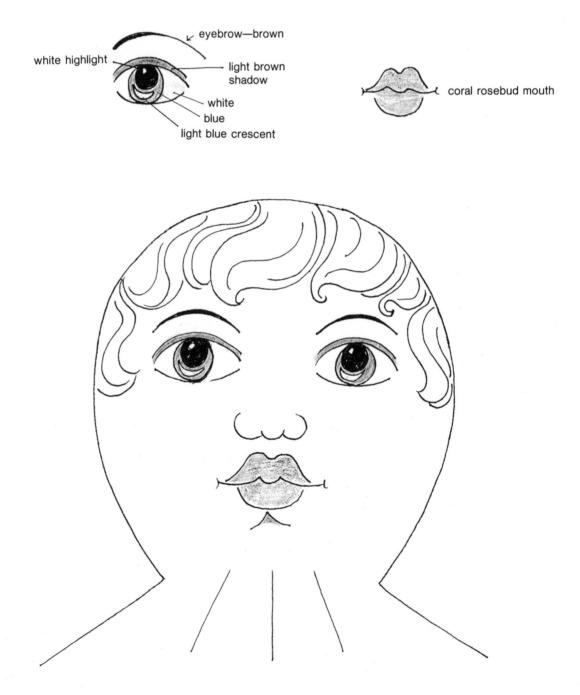

PATTERNS FOR COLUMBIAN DOLL

Note: Enlarge all patterns to correct size by photocopying at 200%, *OR* enlarge by the grid method at 1 cm = 2 cm (½'' = 1'').

Seam allowance of 1 cm (⅜'') is included on all pattern pieces.

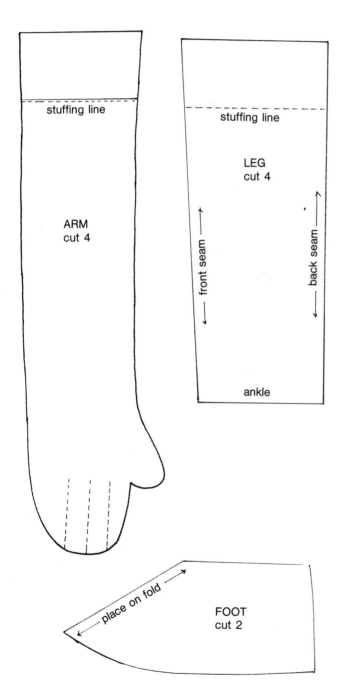

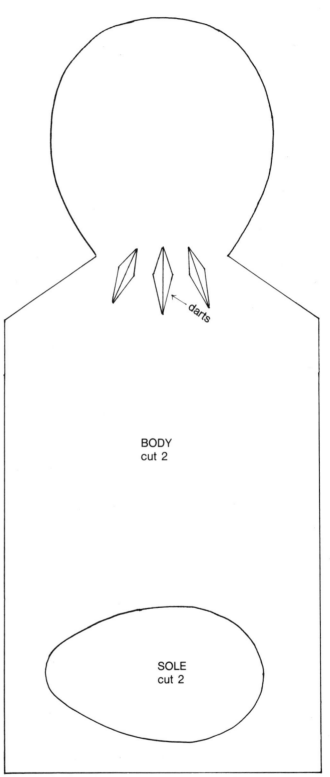

11 Martha Jenks Chase Doll

Illustrated on page 55

MARTHA JENKS CHASE

Born in Pawtucket, Rhode Island in 1851, Martha Jenks married Dr Chase in 1873.

During the latter part of the 1800s and in the early 1900s most dolls on the American market, other than cloth dolls, had bisque heads and composition bodies. They came from Europe, particularly France and Germany. American dollmakers were unable to perfect the technique and doll distributors in the United States, with the assistance of some well known doll designers, had dolls for the American market made and assembled in Europe.

Bisque dolls, which tended to be breakable and relatively heavy, were unsuitable for small children. During this period dollmakers began to search for a more suitable medium.

Martha Chase, like most mothers at the time, was unhappy with the bisque head dolls her three daughters had to play with and dreamed of one that would be soft and cuddly, easy to handle and possibly washable. She made one from stockinet fabric which gained instant popularity among her many friends and their daughters and she found herself busy making dolls as gifts.

She considered stockinet ideal for doll-making, having seen its use in her father's surgery (he was a doctor). It was soft, easy to use and could be stretched as desired. For the head she pressed wet stockinet into a mould and partially filled it with what might have been a mixture of plaster and glue or, more likely, papier-mâché. When the stockinet was removed from the mould she had a mask with features, strong, light and unbreakable.

In 1891 Martha Chase took one of her dolls to Jordan Marsh, a department store in Boston, to be fitted for shoes. The buyer of the doll department was impressed and wanted to place an immediate order. This led to Martha Chase setting up a doll factory at the rear of her house in Pawtucket, which was an instant success. The factory was known as 'The Doll House'.

Assisted by skilled advertising in magazines such as the Ladies Home Journal *and* Vogue, *business was brisk during the years that followed. In 1905 she designed a popular range depicting characters from* Alice in Wonderland *and certain Charles Dickens novels. This was later followed by a George Washington doll.*

In 1911, Martha Chase turned her attention to the health care area, encouraged by both her father and her husband. This led to what was undoubtedly the most important and satisfying achievement of her career. She developed a doll 1.5 m (5 feet tall) for use in hospitals to teach student nurses and doctors methods for the care and handling of patients. In 1913 the Chase Sanitary Doll was introduced to demonstrate infant hygiene in health departments, mothers' clubs and clinics. Both models are still in use all over the world.

Martha Jenks Chase died in 1925.

Materials required

commercial or hand-made head mould 34–35.5 cm (13½''–14'') circumference
0.5 m (½ yd) calico
stuffing
papier-mâché
craft glue
fine sandpaper
acrylic paints (black, white, blue, yellow, flesh)
paint brushes
quick-drying varnish
small length of old ribbon or length of silk frayed to look old
palette knife or ordinary round-pointed knife

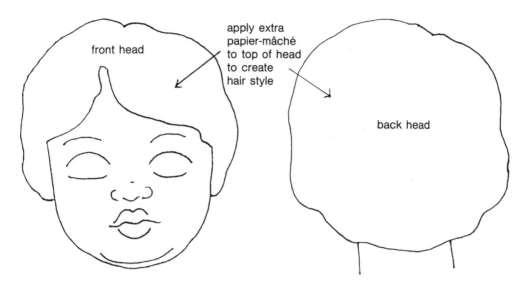

Fig. 1

Head

1. Follow the instructions given for making a head in papier-mâché on pages 8–10.

2. Once the head is dry make up an additional quantity of papier-mâché and, using a knife or palette-knife, place in a thick layer on top of the head. Arrange the material to resemble a bobbed hair design of the 1920s, showing a side parting. See Fig. 1. Leave to dry, then sandpaper the entire head until smooth.

Body

3. Cut out all body pieces in calico, following enlarged patterns from pages 72 and 77. Sew up body and turn right side out, leaving neck open for stuffing. Stuff firmly but without lumps. See Fig. 2.

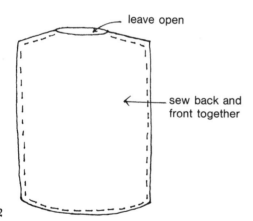

Fig. 2

Arms

4. Sew up lower arms, turn right side out and stuff. Stuff thumbs separately and stitch in place. Sew fingers through from front to back. See Fig. 3. Fold over fabric for tab and machine stitch into tube. Turn right side out.

5. Stuff arms right up to the top and fold over in the same way as wrapping a parcel. Insert tab in the middle and sew together firmly. See Fig. 4.

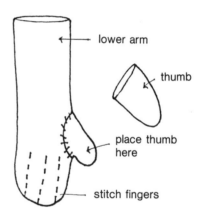

Fig. 3

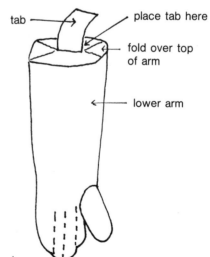

Fig. 4

6. Sew upper arms, turn right side out and stuff. Fold in the ends in the same way as lower arms, inserting the lower arm tab at one end and another tab at the other. Attach arms to body by the upper tab. See Figs 5 and 6.

Legs

7. Sew up centre seam of legs and attach upper feet. Sew back seams, attach soles and turn right side out. Stuff to first stuffing line. Stitch across. Leave a gap and stitch across again at second stitching line. Stuff again to third stitching line. Stitch across. Sew toes and attach legs to body. See Figs 7, 8 and 9.

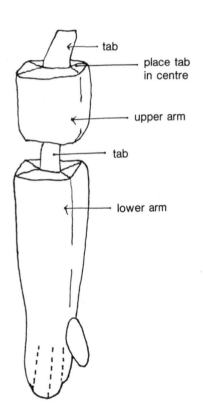

Fig. 5

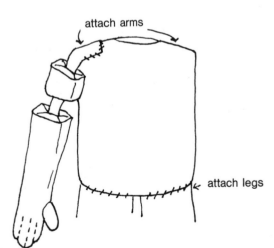

Fig. 6

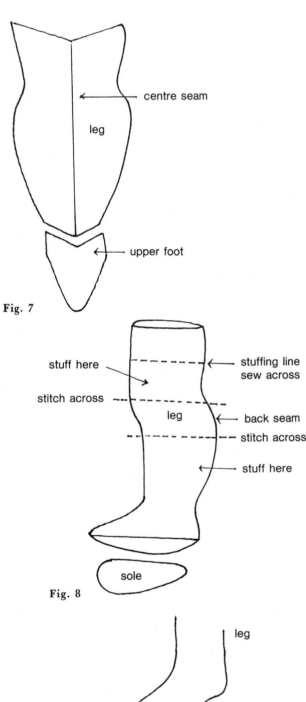

Fig. 7

Fig. 8

Fig. 9

Painting head

8. Paint face, neck and lower arms and legs in flesh. Paint in features following Fig. 10. Allow to dry. Paint hair in yellow using a palette knife to achieve a thick layer (this was the method used by Martha Chase). See Fig. 10.

9. Dry thoroughly and apply two or three coats of varnish.

10. Attach head to top of body either by hand stitching using very strong thread or by gluing into place. See Fig. 10. Make a bow from a length of ribbon or silk and glue to side of head. If possible, old-fashioned printed fabric should be used for the dress.

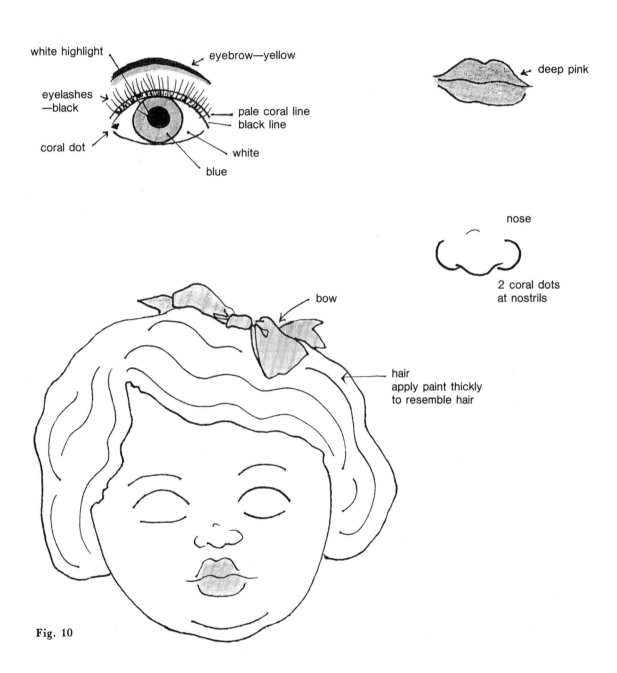

Fig. 10

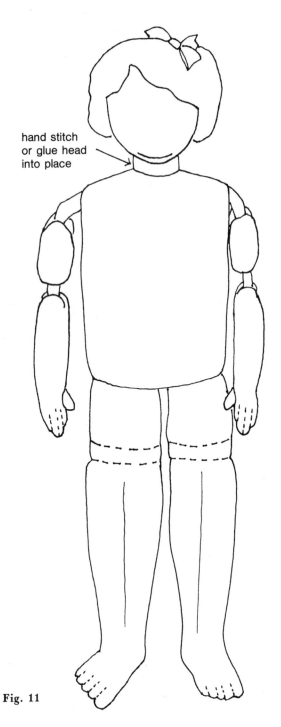

hand stitch
or glue head
into place

Fig. 11

PATTERNS FOR MARTHA JENKS CHASE DOLL

Note: Enlarge all patterns to correct size by photocopying at 200%, *OR* enlarge by the grid method at 1 cm = 2 cm (½'' = 1'').

Seam allowance of 1 cm (⅜'') is included on all pattern pieces.

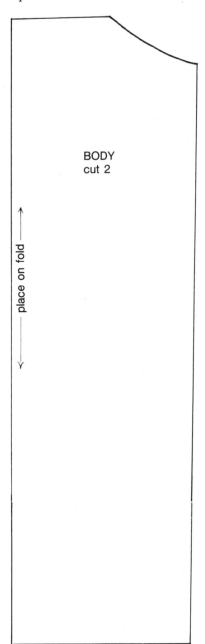

BODY
cut 2

place on fold

Opposite: Reproduction Lenci doll, the 'Art Dolls' of the 1920s (page 59)

Reproduction Alabama Baby with features painted in the extravagant style of some of the porcelain dolls of the early 1900s (page 83)

Bonnet Head Black Baby, a style popular in the 1930s (page 88)

Pooh Bear has been a popular toymaker's subject since the 1920s (page 112)

Reproduction small Steiff bear (page 98), one of many varied Steiff designs

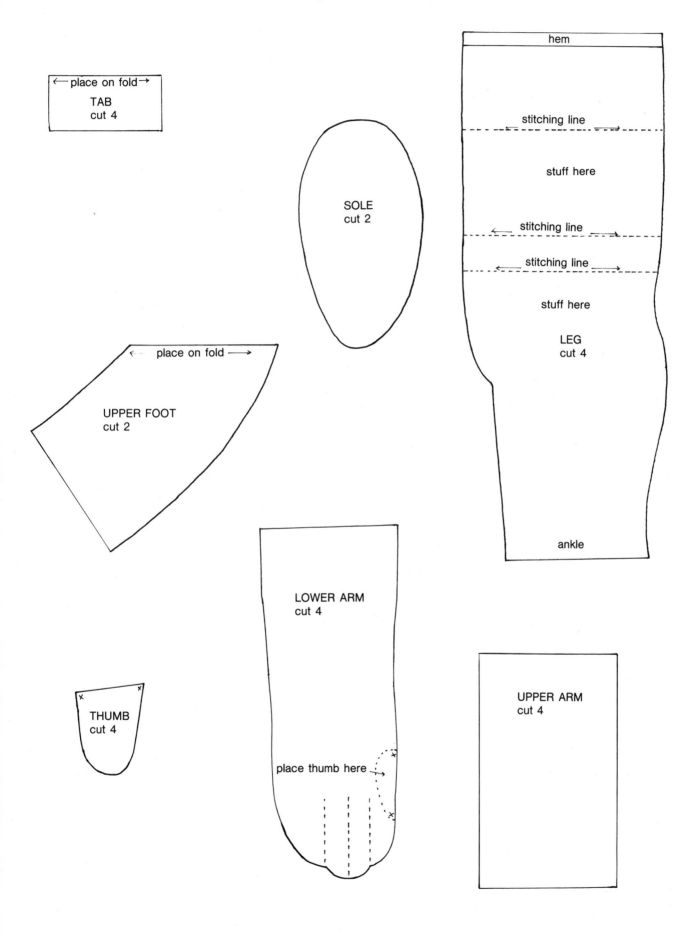

12 Steiff Clown Doll

Illustrated on page 56

MARGARETE STEIFF

The Margarete Stieff dolls are perhaps overshadowed by the attention given over a great many years to the range of bears produced by the same maker but they were original, extremely well-made and displayed their own individuality and attention to detail.

Unlike other contemporary dolls made from felt, velvet or cloth, principally those produced by Lenci and Deans who used 'extras' to make the faces lifelike, Steiff did so by the skilful use of stuffing and the precise and intricate cutting of fabric pieces.

Her factory was established in Geingen, Württemberg, Germany in 1894 and character dolls immediately became a large part of her range. They included policemen, army officers, dwarfs and clowns, among others. 'Outside' workers were employed in the early years, paid on a piece-work basis, but by 1908 her factory work force numbered almost 2000.

On Margarete Steiff's death in 1909 the business was taken over by her nephews who continue to produce well-made dolls and other toys.

A small museum in her birthplace, Geingen, caters to collectors and others who might be interested who call in for advice or simply to admire the museum's collection.

Steiff is dealt with more fully on page 98.

Materials required
0.5 m (½ yd) cream felt for body
white felt for lower legs
black felt for shoes
stuffing
2 small black beads
brown sheep's wool, carded
brown paint
fine brush
craft glue
4 buttons
strong thread or twine
toymaker's needle
fabrics for clothing
coloured wool for pompoms

Head

Note As felt has a tendency to stretch it is always a good idea to tack pieces together before sewing.

1. Cut out head pieces in cream felt. Join lower head to upper head. Fig. 1. Sew the two back head pieces together along the back seam.

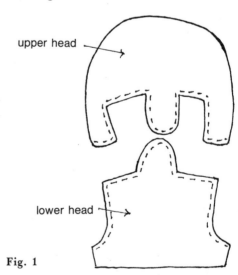

upper head

lower head

Fig. 1

2. Join front of head to back and stuff, leaving neck open. Cut out ears, sew and stuff. Sew to head by hand. Fig. 2.

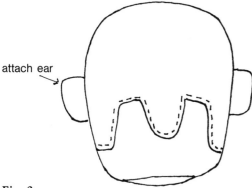

attach ear

Fig. 2

Body

3. Cut out body in cream felt. Sew together and stuff. Fig. 3.

4. Cut out arms in cream felt, sew and stuff. Leave tops open. Sew fingers, stitching through from front to back. Fig. 4.

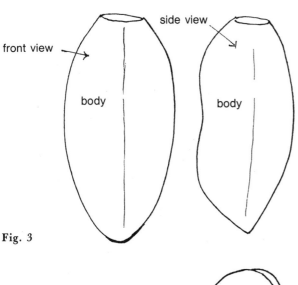

front view

side view

body

body

Fig. 3

leave open

arm

stitch fingers

Fig. 4

Legs

5. There are 4 separate leg pattern pieces. Cut out 4 upper leg pieces in cream felt, 4 lower leg pieces in white felt, 4 foot pieces in black felt and 2 soles in black felt.

6. Sew foot to lower leg. Fig. 5.

7. Sew upper leg to lower leg, then sew front and back seams, leaving top open. Fig. 6. Sew on soles.

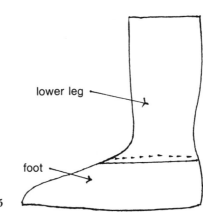

lower leg

foot

Fig. 5

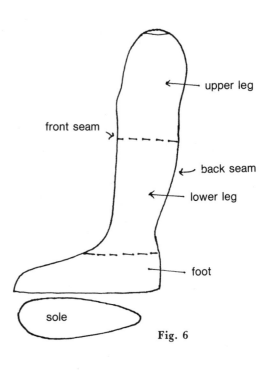

upper leg

front seam

back seam

lower leg

foot

sole

Fig. 6

Attaching arms and legs to body

8. Using a toymaker's needle, insert a double thread or twine and pass needle through body at shoulder level, coming out at the other side and leaving at least

25 cm (10'') of thread at either end. Fig. 7. Tie one end of thread into a loop to prevent thread pulling through. Remove needle at other end, pass thread through 2 holes of button placed inside arm.

Knot tightly to secure.

Complete stuffing of arm and sew up neatly. Undo loop at other end of thread. Place button inside arm. Thread needle and push through arm. Remove needle. Pass thread through button. Fig. 8. Pull as tightly as possible and knot to secure. The arms should be firm against the body but moveable.

9. Attach legs in the same manner. Fig. 8.

Face

10. To make the clown's mouth, using strong thread or twine (without a knot at the end), take needle through back of head to one corner of mouth. Pull thread until end is hidden within head stuffing. Knot at that point. Take thread to other side of mouth and pass needle to back of head. Pull thread tightly and secure with a knot at the back of head. Fig. 9.

11. Sew a black bead on either side of nose for eyes. Fig. 10.

12. Attach head to body with strong thread or twine.

13. Paint eyebrows with brown paint following Fig. 11.

Paint mouth with brown paint to accentuate it. Glue sheep's wool to head for hair.

14. Dress doll in bright colours and trim with pompoms, braid or fancy buttons. Suggested patterns for clown suit and hat are provided. Add large ruffles at neck and sleeves, as in the photograph on page 56.

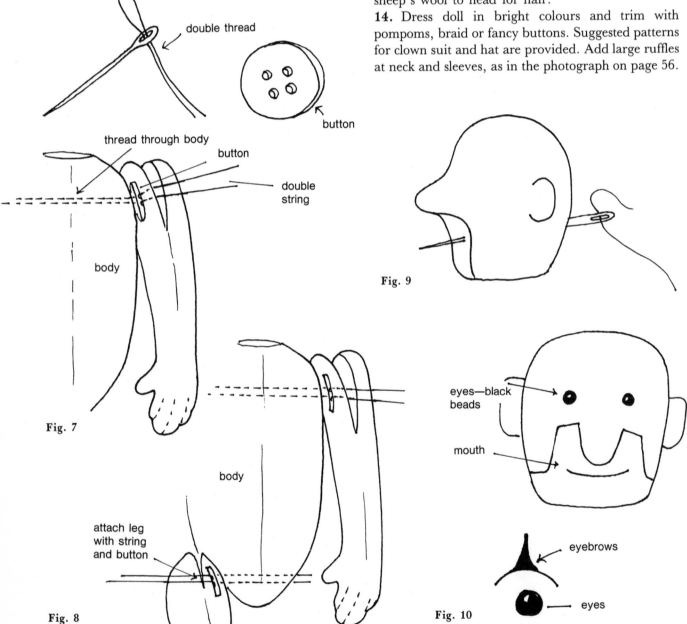

double thread

button

thread through body

button

double string

body

Fig. 7

body

attach leg with string and button

Fig. 8

Fig. 9

eyes—black beads

mouth

eyebrows

eyes

Fig. 10

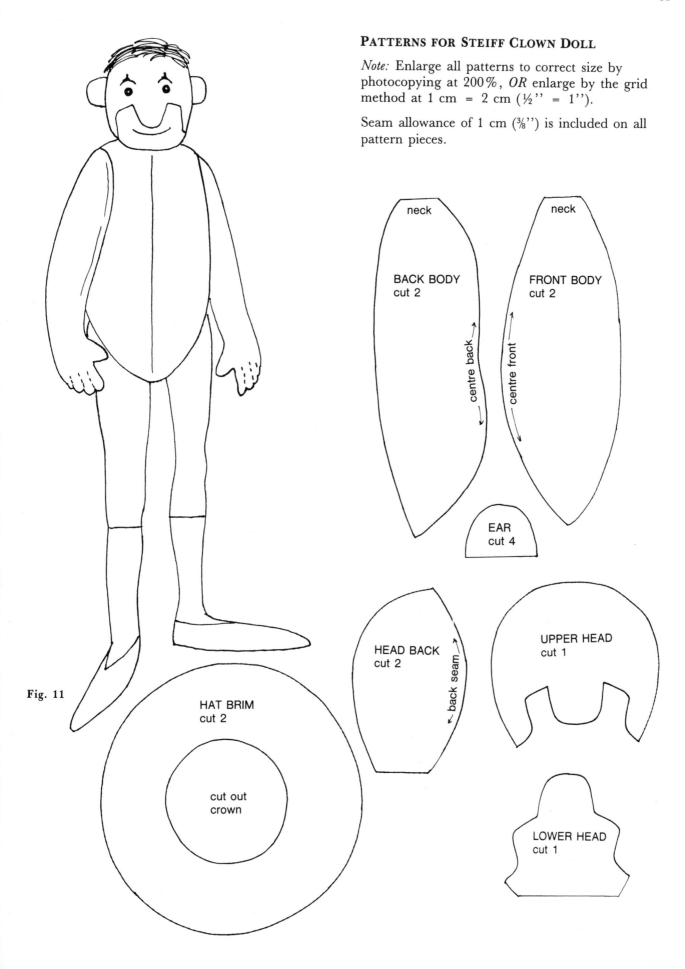

PATTERNS FOR STEIFF CLOWN DOLL

Note: Enlarge all patterns to correct size by photocopying at 200%, *OR* enlarge by the grid method at 1 cm = 2 cm (½'' = 1'').

Seam allowance of 1 cm (⅜'') is included on all pattern pieces.

neck   neck

BACK BODY   FRONT BODY
cut 2   cut 2

centre back   centre front

EAR
cut 4

HEAD BACK   UPPER HEAD
cut 2   cut 1

back seam

HAT BRIM
cut 2

cut out
crown

LOWER HEAD
cut 1

Fig. 11

are available in both short and long pile from most fabric stores. Alternatively, mohair teddy bear fabric, imported from overseas, is easily available and gives an acceptable result.

Since your intention is to fashion an antique looking bear on the lines of a Steiff bear, you would be well advised to obtain some old material. With luck you may find an old fur coat (mohair, camel, wool, etc.) in an op shop or secondhand store. This is the ideal way to go, so have a good try!)

Directions

1. Place enlarged paper patterns from page 102 on the reverse side of the fur fabric and draw around them with a felt-tipped pen, following the pattern check-list. Cut out carefully.

Body

2. Join the two back body pieces together at the centre seam, right sides facing, then join the two front pieces, right sides facing. Stitch back and front together, leaving an opening at the neck. Turn right side out and stuff. Fig. 1.

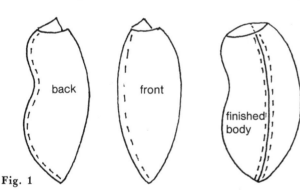

Fig. 1

Arms and legs

3. Cut out paw pads from felt for both arms and legs.
4. Leaving openings at the top, stitch back and front leg sections together. Turn right side out. Tack paw pads to legs to ensure a proper fit, then machine stitch.
5. Follow the same procedure for the arms.
6. Stuff all pieces but leave openings unstitched. Fig. 2.

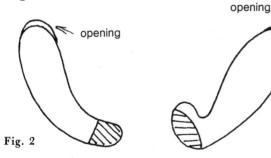

Fig. 2

Head

7. The head is made from three separate pieces. Stitch the side head pieces together from the tip of the nose to the bottom of the neck. Fig. 3.
8. Fit the centre head piece directly to the point of the nose and stitch around both sides. Fig. 4. Turn right side out and stuff.

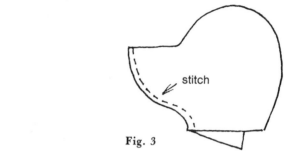

Fig. 3

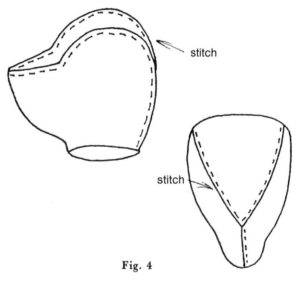

Fig. 4

Joining arms and legs

9. Thread the needle with strong cord doubled; push needle through the bear's body where the arms are to go, leaving a good length of thread each side of the body. Repeat for the legs. Fig. 5.

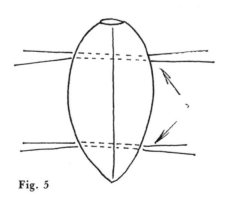

Fig. 5

10. Place a large button inside the arm at the opening. Thread the two strands of cord separately through the holes in the button. Tie a very tight knot.

On the opposite side, pass the cord through the button holes in the same way and pull tightly so that both arms fit tightly against the body. Tie a firm knot. *The arms should not be left to hang loosely.* Fig. 6.

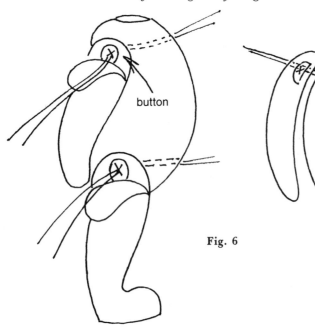

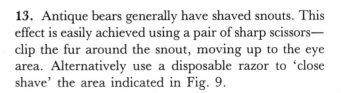

button

Fig. 6

Attach the legs the same way.

Finally, adjust stuffing at top of arms and legs and sew up openings.

A more complex but more authentic way of joining the pieces together is described on pages 104–105.

11. Pin and then stitch the head firmly to the body. Fig. 7.

12. Place ear pieces right sides together and sew by machine. Leave bottom open.

Turn right side out. Turn a narrow hem and attach to head. Do not stuff. Fig. 8.

13. Antique bears generally have shaved snouts. This effect is easily achieved using a pair of sharp scissors— clip the fur around the snout, moving up to the eye area. Alternatively use a disposable razor to 'close shave' the area indicated in Fig. 9.

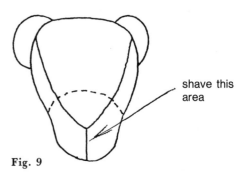

shave this area

Fig. 9

14. Embroider the nose and mouth following Fig. 10 and sew the eyes on firmly.

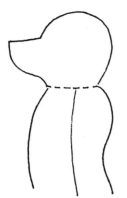

Fig. 7

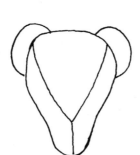

Fig. 8

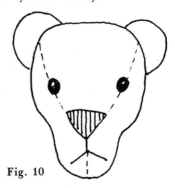

Fig. 10

15. All four paws must be embroidered with claws. Using the same embroidery cotton or wool used for the nose, make three large straight stitches on each paw, going from the underside of the paw to the furry side.

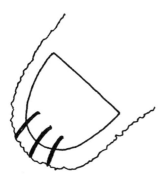

PATTERN CHECK-LIST

This is not a pattern layout, merely a check-list of the pieces involved. Trace the pattern pieces and place the paper patterns on the reverse side of the fabric, arranging them in the most economical manner. Mark around the patterns with a felt-tipped pen. There are 19 pieces cut from fur fabric and 4 pieces (the paw pads) from felt.

Pattern pieces numbered 1–6 must be reversed when cutting in order to fit and 'arm' paw pads from felt must be similarly reversed.

Before laying out the pattern, ensure that the fur pile runs in the right direction. The pile on the arms, legs and body must run from top to bottom. On the two side head pieces the pile must run away from the nose, as it must also on the centre head piece.

PATTERN LAYOUT

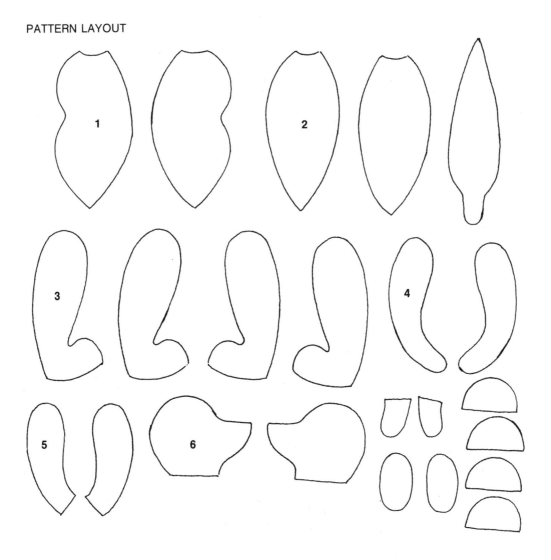

PATTERNS FOR SMALL STEIFF BEAR

Note: Enlarge all patterns to correct size by photocopying at 200%, *OR* enlarge by the grid method at 1 cm = 2 cm (½'' = 1'').

Seam allowance of 1 cm (⅜'') is included on all pattern pieces.

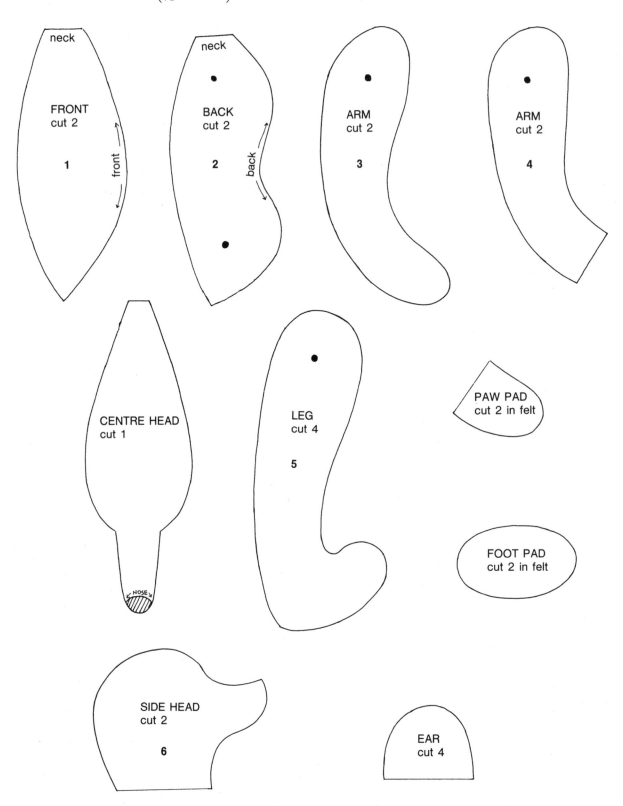

17 Large Steiff Bear

Illustrated on pages 93 and 94

Illustrated on pages 93 and 94

The type of fur used can greatly affect the finished appearance of your bear. Even though the same basic pattern is used, a long-furred bear will look completely different to a short-furred bear, the long pile producing a larger bear.

The Steiff bear described in Chapter 16 is small and the use of short pile fur is preferable. A long pile would alter the shape and, to some degree, the size, while overall the precise lines of a Steiff would no longer be identifiable.

The photographs on pages 93–94, of four bears made to the same large Steiff pattern in different fur fabrics, illustrate this point.

As a general guide, bears less than 30 cm (12'') in height would do well with short pile fabric whereas a long pile would suit larger bears.

The construction of this model and the materials required are essentially the same as those for the small Steiff, so I am not repeating the instructions for cutting out patterns, putting the head and body together, stuffing, joining arms and legs and fixing the eyes and paw pads. It must be emphasised that very special care must be taken in cutting out the patterns, especially when working with long fibre fur fabric. Use your fingers to separate the fibres while cutting and thus avoid damage.

There are some important differences between the two models.

Overall
1. Use a long fibre fur rather than the short fibre used for the small Steiff.

Face
2. Using a sharp pair of scissors and a disposable razor, trim the fur across the entire snout up to the eye area until very little 'fuzz' remains. See Fig. 1.

Nose
3. The nose of this bear is larger and wider than the small Steiff's nose. Follow Fig. 2 and the photographs on pages 93–94 when embroidering the nose.
4. Handsew ears to the head at a 45° angle. See Fig. 3.

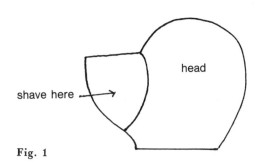

Fig. 1

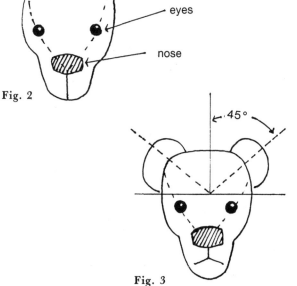

Fig. 2

Fig. 3

Alternative method of attaching arms, legs and head to body

This method is somewhat more complicated than that described on pages 99–100, but its use is recommended since antique bears were generally put together in this way. The arms and legs are attached to the body *before* stuffing begins.

Materials required
5 bolts (or screws) approximately 22 mm long × 5 mm dia (⅞'' × ⅜'')
5 hexagonal nuts or wing nuts to fit
10 washers approximately 30 mm (1⅜'') dia with hole to fit

Note   Plastic joint sets, which include glass eyes, are now available in many craft shops.

1. Leave a part of the back seam of the body open for stuffing. Fig. 1. Turn right side out.

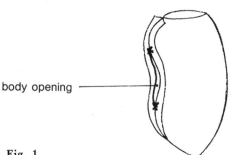

body opening

Fig. 1

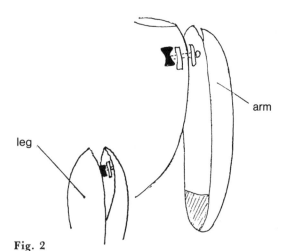

leg

arm

Fig. 2

2. Make a small hole in the bottom half of the body where the leg is to be attached. Working from the *inside* of the body insert a bolt (or screw) through a washer and push it through the hole. Put the bolt (or screw) through a corresponding hole in the inner side of the leg, add another washer and fix a hex or wing nut. Fig. 2.

3. Fig. 3 illustrates the complete bolt assembly.

Tighten the wing nut (or hex nut) until the leg is firm against the body. The joint will be fairly rigid but will loosen directly the body and leg have been stuffed. Each arm and leg is attached separately in this manner.

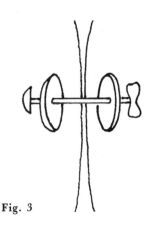

Fig. 3

Head

4. Stuff the head firmly. Place a bolt (or screw), with a washer attached, across the open neck area with the bolt (or screw) protruding outwards. Using a needle and very strong thread, make a running stitch around the neck opening and gather up tightly around the washer. Secure firmly. See Fig. 4.

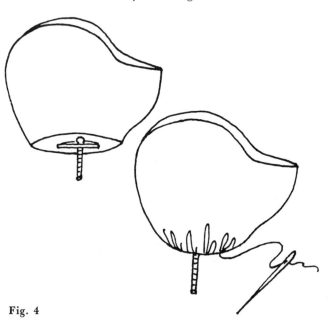

Fig. 4

5. Cut out a circle of fur fabric large enough to fit the body neck opening and sew on to the body by hand. Pass the bolt (or screw) protruding from the head through a hole in the fabric circle and into the body.

Working through the opening at the back of the body, fix a wing (or hex) nut and tighten. Figs 5 and 6.
6. Now stuff the body, arms and legs. Close all openings by hand sewing.

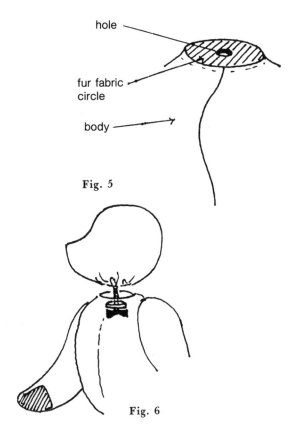

Fig. 5

X = stuffing points before closing seams

Fig. 7

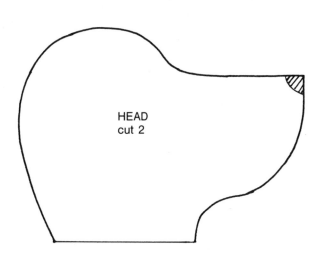

Fig. 6

PATTERNS FOR LARGE STEIFF BEAR

Note: Enlarge all patterns to correct size by photocopying at 200%, *OR* enlarge by the grid method at 1 cm = 2 cm (½'' = 1'').

Seam allowance of 1 cm (⅜'') is included on all pattern pieces.

HEAD
cut 2

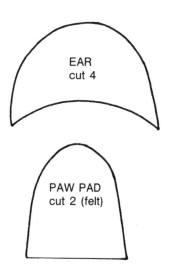

EAR
cut 4

PAW PAD
cut 2 (felt)

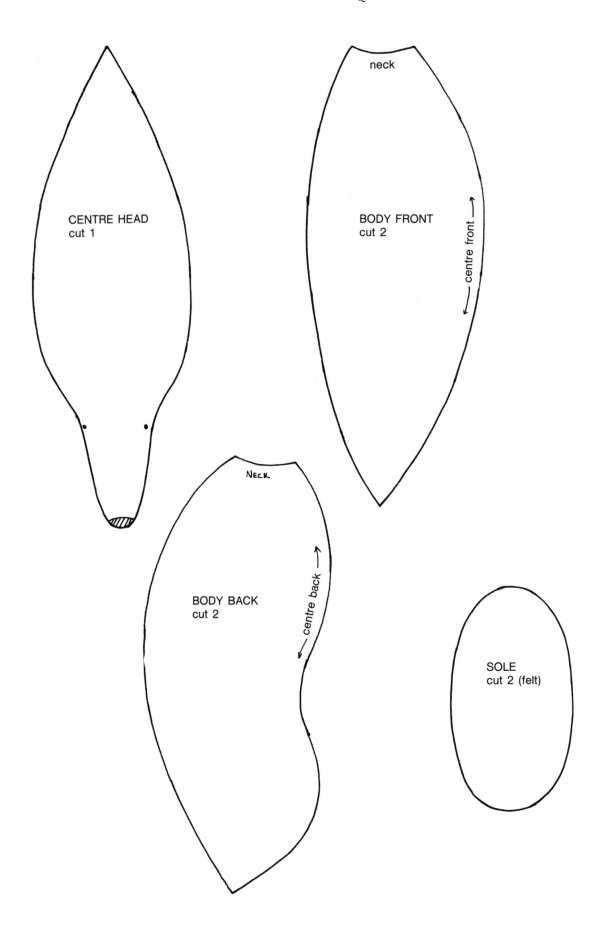

CENTRE HEAD
cut 1

BODY FRONT
cut 2

neck

centre front

BODY BACK
cut 2

Neck

centre back

SOLE
cut 2 (felt)

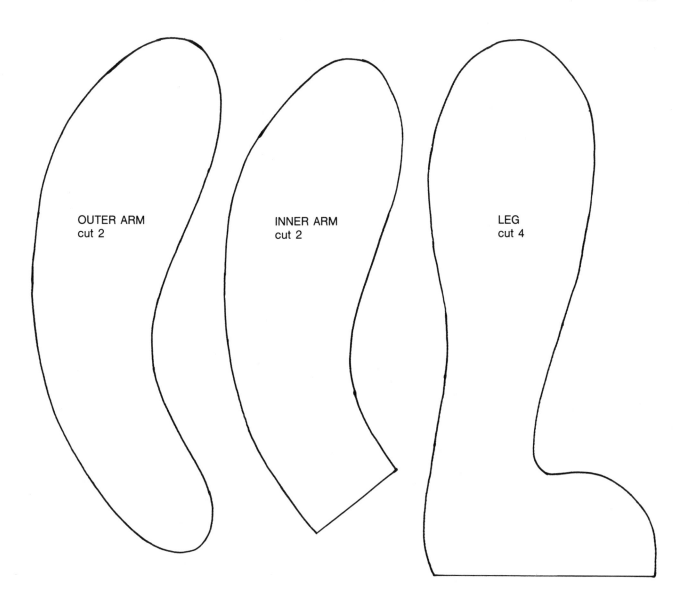

OUTER ARM
cut 2

INNER ARM
cut 2

LEG
cut 4

18 Jester Bear

Illustrated on page 95

Not a great deal is known about the origin of the Jester (or Clown) Bear other than that it was introduced in the 1920s.

The general belief, however, is that the travelling circus, which was a very popular form of entertainment at the time, influenced bearmakers who recognised the commercial potential of such a toy.

It has been suggested that they were either sold outright to circus patrons or used as some form of publicity when the circus came to town.

Steiff continues to manufacture and market the Jester Bear.

Materials required

bear fur fabric

Gold for head, paws and feet

Green for one side of body, one arm and one leg, red for the other side, arm and leg. (If red or green fabrics are not available, light coloured fabric can be dyed with an appropriate fabric dye available from most chemists)

stuffing

pair teddy bear eyes

black embroidery cotton

green wool for pompoms

satin for neck frill

red felt for hat

5 bolts approximately 22 mm long × 5 mm diameter (5½'' × ³⁄₁₆'')

5 wing nuts to suit

10 washers, holes to suit above size, approximately 30 cm (12'') diameter

1. Cut patterns for head, ears, paws and feet in gold fabric. Cut pieces for one arm in red and one leg in green, one leg in red and one arm in green.

2. Cut out pieces for one body back and front in red and one body back and front in green.

Body

3. Sew together one green back and one green front and one red back and one red front. Sew up back and front seams. Leave back open between Xs (see patterns) and neck. Put aside.

4. Attach paws to arms and sew up. Leave top open. Attach feet to legs and sew up. Attach soles. Leave top open. Stuff.

Head

5. Sew side head pieces together from snout down to neck. Sew in head centre. Stuff head firmly down to neck. Insert a bolt and washer inside the head following the instructions on page 104. Using strong thread or twine, gather neck around the bolt and washer and tie off firmly.

6. Pass bolt into body along with a second washer and a wing nut. Tighten wing nut. The back opening makes it easier to fit the head.

7. Attach arms and legs using the bolt and washer method, following the instructions on pages 104–105.

8. Sew ears and stitch to head. Sew on eyes.

9. Embroider nose, mouth and claws with black embroidery cotton following Fig. 1. Stuff the bear and sew up back opening.

Neck frill

10. Measure a length of satin three times neck size and approximately 40 cm (16'') wide. Fold in half to reduce fabric to 20 cm (8'') width.

11. Sew together and turn right sides out. Fold in half and gather to fit around neck.

12. Make four pompoms using patterns provided.

13. Cut hat pattern in red felt, two for the hat and two for the lining. See Figs 1 and 2.

14. Sew hat to lining leaving a small section open at the base (brim). Turn right side out. Sew up opening by hand. Turn brim up as shown in photograph on page 95 and see Figs 3 and 4.

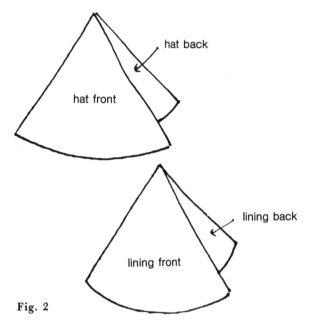

Fig. 2

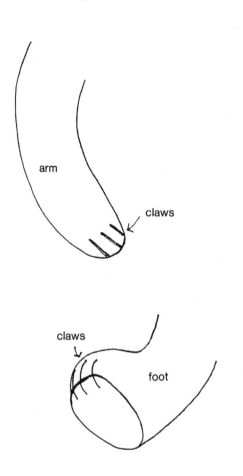

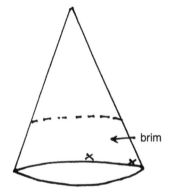

Fig. 3

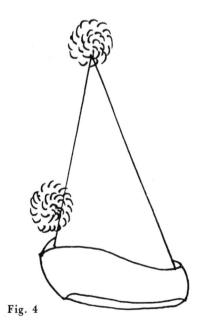

Fig. 4

Fig. 1

PATTERNS FOR JESTER BEAR

Note: Enlarge all patterns to correct size by photocopying at 200%, *OR* enlarge by the grid method at 1 cm = 2 cm (½'' = 1'').

Seam allowance of 1 cm (⅜'') is included on all pattern pieces.

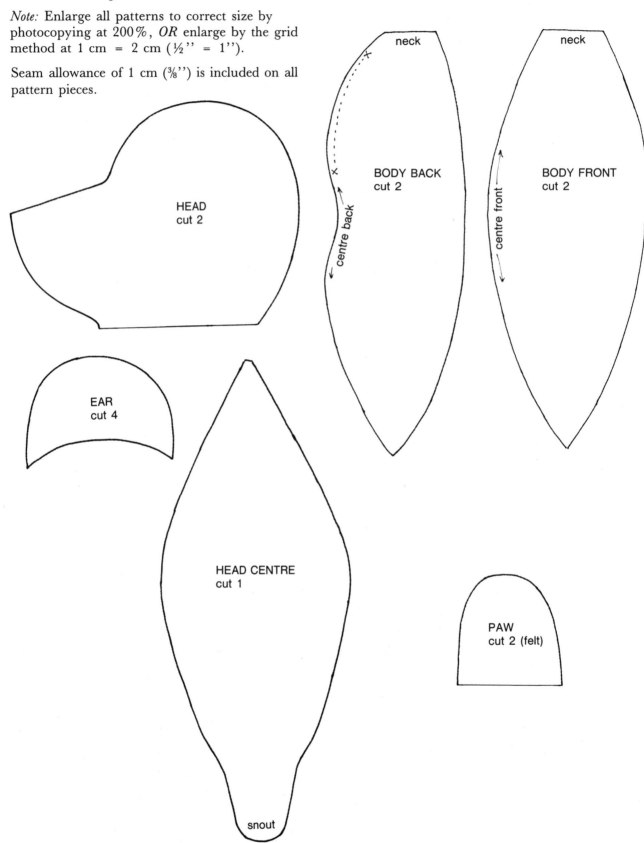

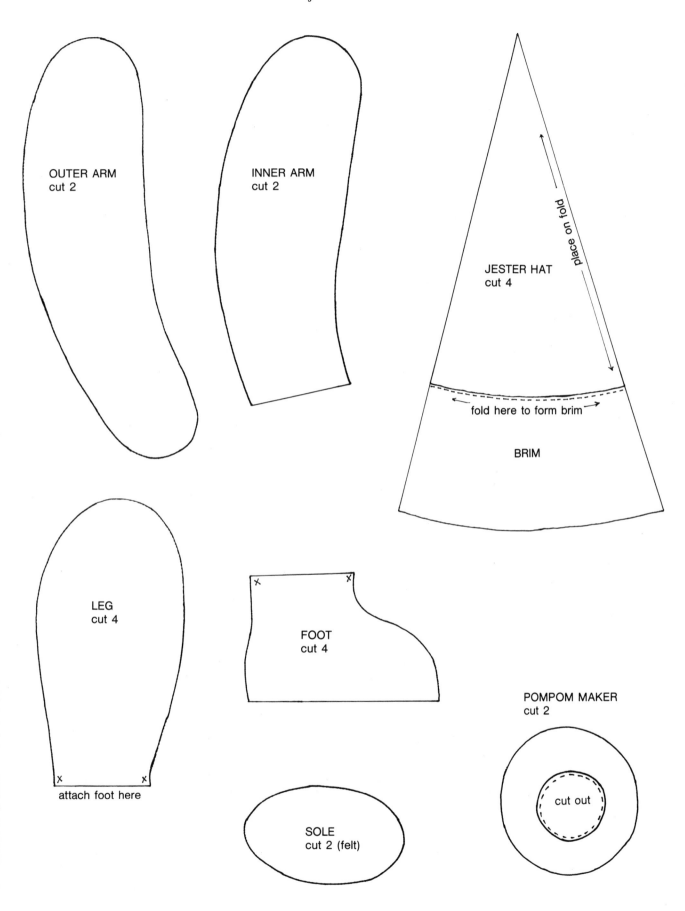

19 Pooh Bear

Illustrated on page 76

EDWARD BEAR

> *Our Teddy Bear is short and fat,*
> *Which is not to be wondered at.*
> *A bear, however hard he tries,*
> *Grows tubby without exercise.*

This was Edward Bear, alias Winnie the Pooh, now known to all bear lovers as Pooh Bear, brought to life for adults and children alike in A.A. Milne's classic books published in the 1920s.

There appears to be no record of any individual bearmaker having exclusive rights to manufacture Pooh Bear, and thousands were produced during the many years that followed.

In 1976, Pooh's fiftieth birthday was celebrated in England with all the pomp and ceremony of such occasions. The original Pooh was sent out from the United States as the principal guest!

Pooh is still with us today and can be visited at the Central Children's Room of the New York Public Library.

Using these patterns, and following the assembly instructions in previous chapters, give yourself the pleasure and satisfaction of putting together what is probably the most famous bear in English literature.

PATTERNS FOR POOH BEAR

Note: Enlarge all patterns to correct size by photocopying at 200%, *OR* enlarge by the grid method at 1 cm = 2 cm (½'' = 1'').

Seam allowance of 1 cm (⅜'') is included on all pattern pieces.

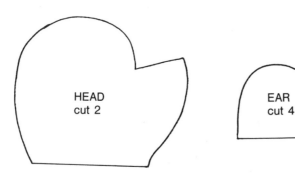

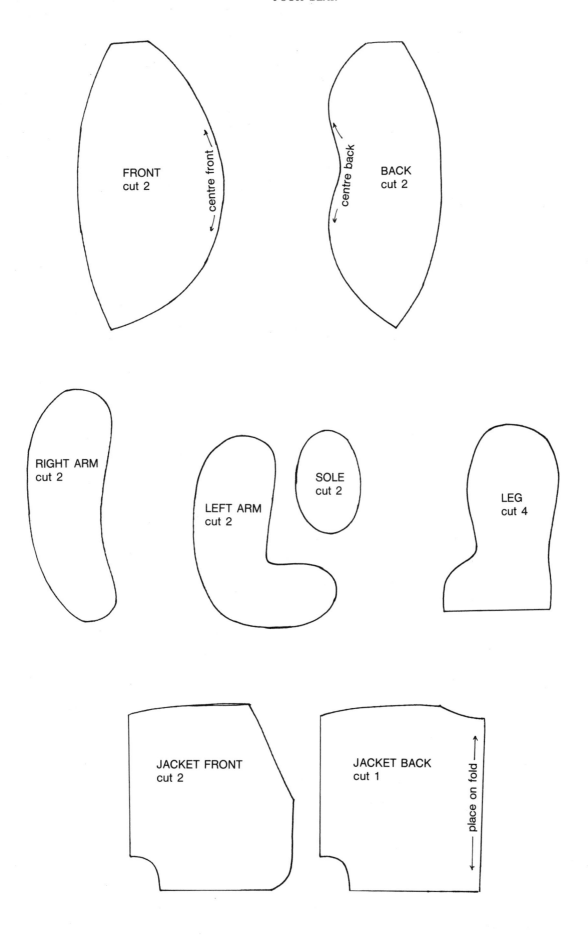

FRONT
cut 2

centre front

BACK
cut 2

centre back

RIGHT ARM
cut 2

LEFT ARM
cut 2

SOLE
cut 2

LEG
cut 4

JACKET FRONT
cut 2

JACKET BACK
cut 1

place on fold

20 Threadbears

Illustrated on page 96

These are old-fashioned bears, not quite antiques, but excellent examples to add to your collection which at the same time will improve your competence at bear-making.

While the overall construction technique is the same as for the other bears in this book, the object here is to transform their finished appearance, to make them threadbare, to give them that 'old' look—well worn and loved to death!

Using a sharp disposable razor, shave areas of the bear's coat as closely as possible—around, for instance, the snout,

ears, elbows, tummy and paws and not forgetting the bottom, probably the first spot that would begin to show wear.

You could go one step further and use a pair of scissors or a sharp knife to make small incisions here and there, pull some stuffing out far enough to be seen, and sew up the hole again with stitches that remain visible, as if a child had done the job. Patches are another good idea.

The intention is to spoil their new-made look, but how far you go with it is entirely up to your discretion.

The three bears in this chapter are bears of quite different characters; you can even use them to make 'unthreadbears', as the variation of Threadbear I on page 96 shows.

Threadbear I

PATTERNS

Note: Enlarge all patterns to correct size by photocopying at 200%, *OR* enlarge by the grid method at 1 cm = 2 cm (½'' = 1'').

Seam allowance of 1 cm (⅜'') is included on all pattern pieces.

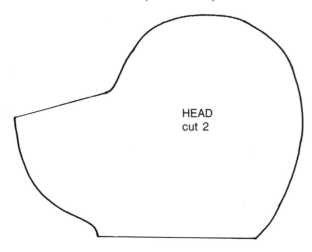

HEAD
cut 2

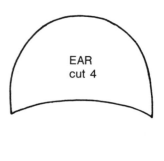

EAR
cut 4

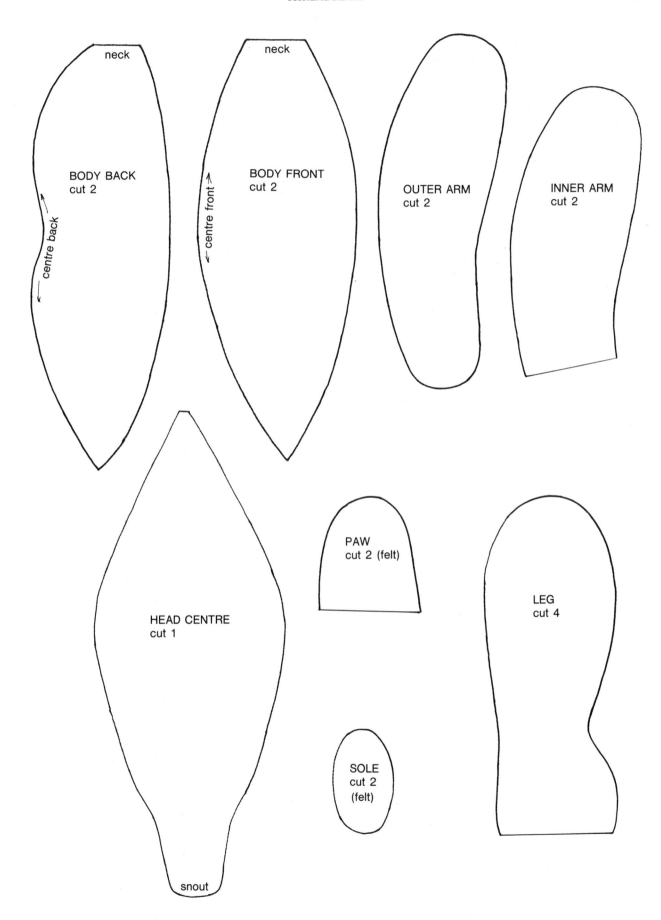

Threadbear II

PATTERNS

Note: Enlarge all patterns to correct size by photocopying at 200%, *OR* enlarge by the grid method at 1 cm = 2 cm (½'' = 1'').

Seam allowance of 1 cm (⅜'') is included on all pattern pieces.

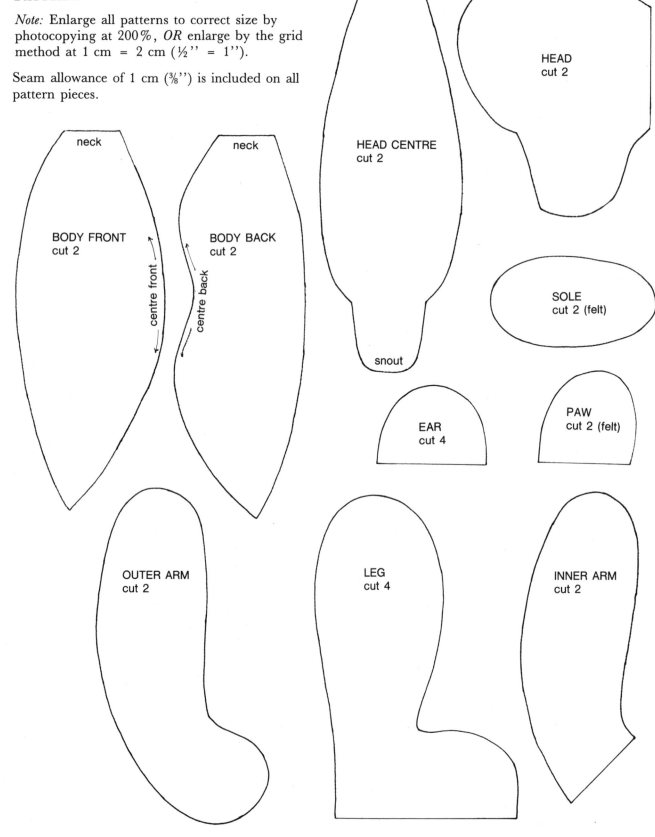

Threadbear III

PATTERNS

Note: Enlarge all patterns to correct size by photocopying at 200%, *OR* enlarge by the grid method at 1 cm = 2 cm (½'' = 1'').

Seam allowance of 1 cm (⅜'') is included on all pattern pieces.

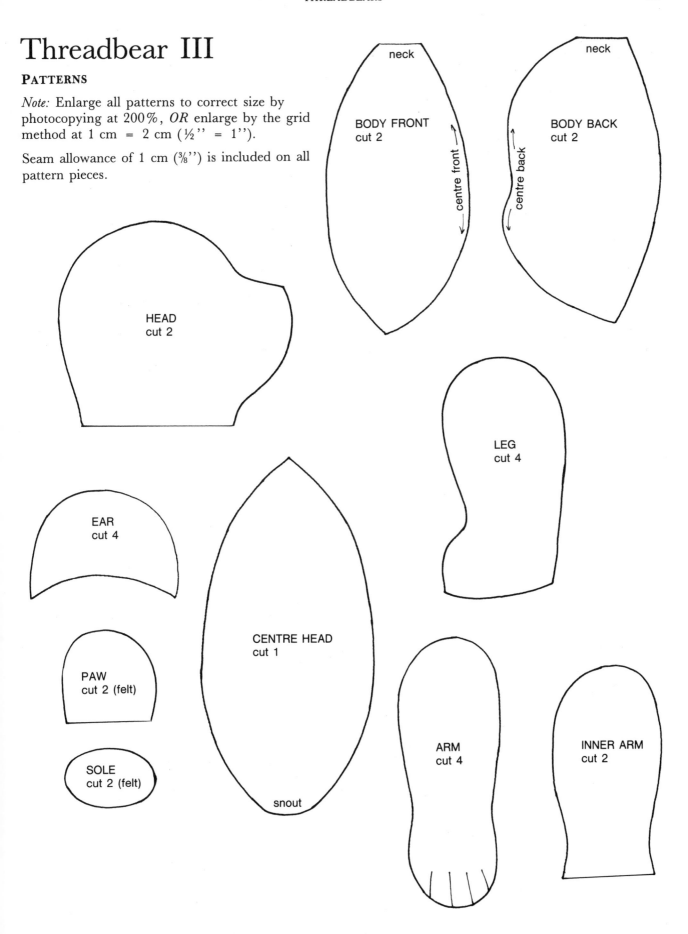

INDEX